THE LAYMAN'S GUIDE TO THE 48 ACTS

L K TAYLOR

With love and gratitude; To those I have loved, and to those who have loved me.

I would like to thank and pay gratitude to all the Scientists, Medics, Philosophers, Mystics and Spiritual Gurus, whose works I have read, and whose workshops and study days I have attended. Your names are too numerous to mention but your inspiration is everywhere to be seen throughout this book.

CONTENTS

THE LAYMAN'S GUIDE: PART ONE

"It is not what you are looking at, it is how you are looking at it."	3
Our Brain	35
What Happens Next?	41
Understanding	47
In A More Layman's Language	49
Anxiety: The Greatest Problem Of The Twenty-First Century	53

THE LAYMAN'S GUIDE TO THE SIXTEEN AXIOMS

Act 1	61
Act 2	65
Act 3	71
Act 4	77
Act 5	81
Act 6	87
Act 7	91
Act 8	95
Act 9	99
Act 10	101
Act 11	103
Act 12	107
Act 13	111
Act 14	113
Act 15	117
Act 16	119

THE LAYMAN'S GUIDE TO THE "SIXTEEN FALSE BELIEFS"

Act 1	125
Act 2	129
Act 3	131
Act 4	133

Act 5	135
Act 6	139
Act 7	143
Act 8	145
Act 9	147
Act 10	149
Act 11	153
Act 12	157
Act 13	161
Act 14	165
Act 15	169
Act 16	171

THE LAYMAN'S GUIDE TO THE "SIXTEEN KEY ACTIONS"

Act 1	177
Act 2	179
Act 3	183
Act 4	187
Act 5	191
Act 6	209
Act 7	213
Act 8	215
Act 9	217
Act 10	219
Act 11	223
Act 12	227
Act 13	229
Act 14	231
Act 15	233
Act 16	235
Footnote	237

THE LAYMAN'S GUIDE:
PART ONE

"IT IS NOT WHAT YOU ARE LOOKING AT, IT IS HOW YOU ARE LOOKING AT IT."

I have spent an entire lifetime living and working in highly anxious environments.
    I have worked in some of the most highly volatile and dangerous places on the planet.

I have sat and listened to people in some of their darkest and most challenging moments.

I have wanted to die, and have tried to die.

I have spent huge chunks of my life acquiring knowledge and information on just about every aspect of the human condition, just so I could survive.

Survive what, you might ask? Honestly? I never really knew the answer.

Seven years ago, the chaos that was my life enveloped me in the most unimaginable darkness, and I almost did not make it. Except for the love of family and close friends, and the wonderful expertise of medics, I would have become another statistic of the modern cancer of suicide.

I am now seven years into the journey of trying to make sense of my story of life. Understanding our stories may be coupled with terror, fear, shame, guilt and hurt, but they also bring hope, compassion, love and freedom.

It was during this period of time, while I was at my lowest point, that I came across Paddy Rafter and his work *The 48 Acts* or as it was called at that time *The 48 Acts Towards A New Way of Living*. It was almost as if Paddy was telling me my own story, but the difference was that he was telling me my story in a way that made sense to me for the very first time. It had a profound effect on me. As I mentioned earlier, over a lifetime I had acquired vast amounts of knowledge, information and experience through study and in my professional capacity, but the one piece I was missing was awareness. An awareness of me. I was aware of just about everything and everybody else, but I had no awareness of myself.

The topics that Paddy speaks about, like our programming, environments, and the different types of environments that make up and impact the world, really began to resonate with me.

These are some of the different types of environments he describes; Internal human environment of self, environment of family, external environment of community, society, planet.

He speaks about how the balance of all these environments are essential for the well-being of society and our planet.

He speaks about the energy of the universe and how that energy and divine spark are present in every one of us.

The one thing that jumped out for me was how the microcosm of self has an impact (negative or positive) on the well-being of the macrocosm of society.

He speaks about our faulty programming and our addiction to the drugs of approval and appreciation.

He speaks about how our species is so deprived of gut and instinctual knowing.

He speaks about how fear and anxiety are destroying the ecosystem of the human species.

But more than anything else, he speaks about truth and reality. The only way to achieve wellness is to live in reality and to learn to live with truth, in a world where truth is an ever-declining fact.

Paddy's awareness, his ability to take personal responsibility for his own story and difficulties, and a very unique understanding of a very troubled world, have allowed me for the first time to take all the knowledge and information that I have learned, and through the telling of my own story, create an awareness of myself that I would not have had heretofore.

Telling my story through a lifetime of acquired knowledge and information, and most recently awareness of myself through Paddy Rafter's *The 48 Acts Towards a New Way of Living*.

But first my story.

I was born in a middle-sized provincial Irish town. I was the third of five children, and our family lived in a working-class area. The local neighborhoods were very vibrant, and there was a great sense of community. We knew all of our neighbors and their families, and we spent most of our free time playing outside.

We would stay out playing in the evenings, particularly during the summer months when the daylight lasted several hours longer, and often we only went home when we were hungry.

We often went to other kids' houses to play, although they must have noticed that it was very seldom, they were invited to play in our house. We simply could not ask them. Our house was too unpredictable—because my mother suffered from a debilitating condition known in those days as manic-depressive psychosis (now called bipolar disorder), and my father's way of coping with it was to retreat to the pub next door, often for hours at a time.

One result of his heavy drinking was that when Ireland sank into a deep recession in the early 1970s, which hit his family business very hard, he fell into debt. So, after his parents died, we moved into their house, and our house was sold to pay off some of the debt. Although it was only three doors down from where we had been living, the difference was drastic.

For one thing, the house was in a state of utter disrepair. It was cold and damp, and there was no escaping the water from above or below.

Every time it rained outside, it also rained inside our house through holes in the roof, so there would be pots and basins everywhere to collect it. The foundation of this house was ten feet lower than our old one—in fact it was even lower than the river itself—so during the winter months the ground floor was regularly flooded. Even when the water receded, there was a persistent dampness throughout the house, so the wallpaper was always peeling and the corners of the linoleum in the kitchen always curled. The cost of renovating it was too high, and anyway the money was simply not there. For my parents there was a lot of shame, which was well-hidden.

Our home was always a place of high anxiety and uncertainty because of our family dynamics, but in many ways I would rather have spent my days there than having to go to school, which for me was torture right from the start.

That was because at a mere five years of age I began to develop a paralyzing fear of being anything less than perfect. This was partly thanks to a nun who was my teacher for my first three years of primary school, which I spent at the local convent.

Like many nuns at the time, she was utterly intimidating, an imposing figure draped in a full black robe, with a huge set of rosary beads wrapped around her waist. Her voice was gentle enough in her regular speech, but when she shouted you could hear her for quite a distance.

She carried a ruler inside a giant pocket in her robe, and it was not to teach us measurements. Her great mission was to instill in us the catechism, a set of questions and answers on the teachings of the Roman Catholic Church, and if that meant having to use the ruler—well then, so be it. The questions were color-coded for different degrees of difficulty, and we had to learn them verbatim. Any mistakes would be met with a slap of the ruler.

I learned to try to be perfect in order to avoid punishment, and I did mostly manage to escape punishment by memorizing, memorizing, memorizing, unlike some of my more unfortunate classmates.

I got great respite the following year when I moved up to the Christian Brothers Primary School for second class, and had a lovely young teacher not long out of teacher training. In addition to being a charismatic teacher and a gentleman, he also shared with us a love of theatre and drama. My brother and I were both in his class, and he wrote a play with us in mind for the starring roles. Written in Irish and called "The Bonanza Kid", it was a western about a local sheriff and an outlaw who looked an awful lot like each other, resulting in comedic cases of mistaken identity.

It was quite literally my first pronounced role as the good child, as I was cast as the sheriff who kept law and order. It did wonders for my sense of self and my general well-being.

In all other aspects of my life, I hardly said a word, to such an extent that my father called me "the listener". I was the observer, the quiet one, standing back and listening as I constantly anticipated danger, while also being afraid of saying the wrong thing.

Yet walking out on the stage was fantastic, because the character had a voice. Even as a young child, I had a strong sense that I could identify with characters, so it was easy to get into the skin of what they were supposed to be. It was also great to take on the persona of someone else, because that meant not having to be myself.

Third class in primary school was where my life was to change forevermore. I was sexually abused for a period of about nine months by a person in a position of trust outside the family. The abuse stopped when I got my summer holidays at the end of third class.

Throughout that summer I suffered with extreme nightmares, night tremors and bed wettings. I would wake up in the middle of the night screaming and unable to breathe.

My mother would call the doctor to come in the middle of the night, and I was eventually diagnosed as having asthma. Strangely enough, I never seemed to have asthma attacks during the day; it was only in the middle of the night.

Of course, we now know it was panic attacks I was experiencing. I eventually told my mother what had happened to me out of pure terror and fear, as I was going back to school in September.

I know that my mother went into the school to speak to somebody, but to this day I have no idea what happened, as it was never spoken about again. My mother told me that I would be going back to school and assured me that everything would be okay. She was right to the extent that the abuse stopped, but I did not realize back then how the experience was going to shape and define my entire life afterwards.

The rest of my school years passed by in a blur. I was always on the outside looking in. I was never involved in team sports of any sort. I developed a way of staying detached from everything and everybody; in that way I could never get hurt, and nobody would ever find out what my secret was. I really do not remember happiness, but I do not remember sadness either. I always remained in that neutral, almost numb state. I just remember my school days as a time of high anxiety, and I experienced my education through fear.

A lot of my teachers were strict disciplinarians with a fondness for the leather strap. Some would give us lashings on the hand for not sitting up, for being untidy, for not doing homework, and for that all-encompassing category: being unruly. This environment for me meant a constant fear, all day every day, of being punished for imperfection. It is very hard even now to describe what that fear meant, other than a constant feeling like a hole in the pit of my stomach, and an ongoing sense of impending doom: an expectation that something bad was going to happen, but never knowing what that something bad actually was. This for me was crucifying as I already felt dirty and bad inside, and any slap from a leather strap only re-enforced what I already knew anyway, and pushed my dirty little secret deeper inside me.

I learned to use denial and pretense as protection. *If I don't pay attention, then I can continue my life unnoticed. I can make the world safe in my own head. I can make myself invisible to harm.* I desperately wanted to be someone who fit in, who was not plagued by the idea of being different, or being flawed. Essentially, I just wanted to be valued and loved.

I did not know that fears kept hidden only become fiercer. I did not know that my habits of pleasing, placating, and pretending were only making me worse. None of my learning through fear led to a broadening of the mind or a thirst for knowledge, naturally. All it did was breed anxiety. I, as a rule follower, did my best to avoid punishments. I also harbored a secret wish that my doing well in school would make me feel like somebody and take away the deep sense of darkness.

Some of my teachers did pick up on this, or at least hints of it. Their typical refrain at teacher/parent meetings about me was, "Has potential, could be better." And I distinctly remember one of the Christian Brothers telling my mother that I was highly intelligent, but was underachieving. If only he had known. If only I could have told someone what I was feeling.

None of that really made a difference, as I had decided to join the army, and back in those days you did not need an education to join the army. That took away the pressure when I sat my Leaving Certificate exams at the end of secondary school, as I knew I would be setting off to training in a couple of months' time regardless of what my scores were.

It did not take away my anxiety and fear of imperfection, though. That was something that I would carry with me into my army experience and beyond.

GROWING UP IN A UNBALANCED ENVIRONMENT

I joined the army to spite my mother. I also did it to escape from our family and to join a new, larger family in which I would be able to hide because no one there knew me—and paradoxically, at the same time to rise above the rest and become somebody.

I did not have a clue who that somebody might be, but in my school days I would daydream and dream at night about becoming somebody special who would grow up to make a difference in the world. Some kids wanted to be pop stars, or film stars or sports heroes. I just wanted to be someone other than me. I knew that my mother would not approve of my choice of joining the army.

It wasn't that I didn't love my mother; in fact, I loved her profoundly, even though in our family we did not express anything of the sort at that time.

Throughout my childhood she suffered from a severe manic-depressive psychosis—and because she suffered so much, we all suffered along with her. I carried a deeply-rooted guilt through most of my life, that in some way I had made my mother's sickness worse because of what happened to me.

She was born in the West of Ireland. The second youngest of a large family, she was highly intelligent and went on to study medicine in college.

In her teenage and young adult years she suffered with what would have been euphemistically known as "the nerves", but still managed to persevere through her studies and function on some level.

My dad had left school early, and worked in the family business. He met my mother at a dance in the local ballroom, where many romances began in Ireland. They got married, and within eight years they had five children. Although she wanted to have a family, that was a lot to handle in quick succession, and she experienced several miscarriages as well.

I was, of course, too young to know from personal experience, but that rapid change in her life and level of responsibility, plus the emotional fortitude needed to raise a young family, while also being geographically removed from her own family, no doubt took its toll on her already struggling mental well-being.

All my mother ever wanted to do was die, and I could never figure that out. She would often say to us that she could never really explain to us what she was experiencing. The only way she had of expressing it was: "I would give anything to be sitting here dying of heart disease or cancer, because then I would have a name for it and I would know what it was".

But she could not find a name for that awful loneliness and emptiness that she was experiencing constantly. Instead, she would constantly complain about her condition. About my father's drinking —she was always a victim, telling us, "You don't know" or "you don't care". She always spoke about "going to the river".

When I was growing up, she was always sick, either mentally or physically. Our home was a highly anxious environment, an anxiety that spilled over into my existence outside the house as well. It all served to make my mind utterly unsettled, so that I was always waiting for something to go wrong, even though it was not that bad all the time, the truth was that you could never trust that things were going to be okay.

During the day, instead of being able to focus on the lessons at school, my brain would be in turmoil, anticipating that everything would not be okay when I got home, because we never knew what would be coming next. Would she be high? Would she be in bed? Would she be low? Would she be there at all? Trying to concentrate on our school lessons, I would find myself utterly disconnected, chunks of time passing by after which I would realize that I had not absorbed a word the teacher had said.

Then, at night, we waited for my father to come home after the pub. Starting at a very young age, I would lie, flat on my back, staring at the ceiling as the minutes and hours ticked by, and worry about the argument that could potentially kick off when my father walked through the door. And although there were many nights when there were no arguments, the reality was that you were always waiting for it to happen. The fear wasn't that he would be obnoxious or angry, or that he would become violent—he was totally the opposite, he was a very quiet and passive man. It was my mother who would do the shouting at him.

To make matters worse, on the nights that I would somehow get to sleep, I would have terrible nightmares and tremors, and would often wake up with awful panic attacks and bed-wetting. It was around this time that I became my mother's closest listener and confidant. I could sit for hours listening to her vent her feelings and frustrations, and giving out about my father's drinking. I used to find it strangely comforting to live in my mother's dark world, as it became a distraction from the almost constant inner darkness that I was experiencing. In some ways it became a gift that I brought through life afterwards, an ability to live in and understand other people's darkness.

However, I was to discover many years later that you cannot hide from your own darkness, and that at some point and time it will catch up with you. To make matters worse, I thought I was the only one in our family who was unable to overcome that anxiety, because everybody else appeared to be handling things quite well, but I discovered as the years went by that that was not the case.

I went to bed every night dreaming that I would grow up and be some sort of a superhero that could fix the world, and that mammies should not have to suffer like my mammy, and that little boys should not have to go to bed with such fear and anxiety.

One of my worst Christmas memories is from a Christmas Eve night when I was around ten or eleven years old, and when (I am not proud to admit) I even wished my mother was dead. Christmas Eve in our house was never a happy occasion to begin with, as it was always shrouded in anxiety, depression and alcohol, and it was often the time of the year that my mother would be at her lowest. So, for about three weeks before Christmas I would worry about what was going to happen. *Will mammy be okay? Will Santa come? Will daddy be in the pub?* I would pray and pray for a normal Christmas.

On this Christmas Eve night I remember being the only one in the house aside from my mother. My father was in the pub, which was a mere two doors away from our house. I was sitting in the kitchen. My mother had been in bed all day with a bad migraine, but suddenly I heard her bedroom door open, and she came rushing down the staircase and into the kitchen. She was in her nightgown and robe, and in a very high manic state, squealing that either daddy came home from the pub, or she was "going to the river".

She caught me by the hand, went out the front door, and brought me into the pub where my father was. She started screaming incoherently in the middle of the packed pub about what my father's drinking was doing to her, and that if he did not come home, she would go to the river. I do not think that I have ever experienced such shame, humiliation and embarrassment, as well as fear and terror, in all my life. It was over as quickly as it happened. My father brought us home, and I went to bed, not that there was any chance of sleeping. I remember lying there and thinking that my mother would do everybody a favor if she did go to the river and die, for maybe that would have brought peace to the house.

The guilt that I carried with me through life afterwards—that I was capable of thinking that way about my mother—was incredible.

"THE MENTAL"

When my mother was really unwell, she would be taken to "The Mental", a public psychiatric hospital in our town. When my mother was there, I always felt a huge sense of guilt, because I always felt as a child that mammy was unwell because of my secret. It was miserable for her to go there, miserable for my father to have to bring her there, and miserable for us to visit.

Still, I made regular visits to see my mother, even though no one ever forced us to go. My father or one of my older siblings might take me up there in my younger years, and from around the age of twelve I would walk up on my own to visit her. In truth I hated going in there with a passion, but I felt obligated to do so.

And so once or twice a week I would walk the fifteen-minute journey to the hospital, and then sit there in a chair beside the bed, or side by side with her on the corridor, or looking out the window in the common room, until I felt that enough time had passed that it was okay to leave.

I might have uttered a simple hello as I entered, but we never exchanged a hug or other pleasantries, and for my entire time there we would sit, showing no emotion, in total silence. Every minute was agony. An hour there was the maximum I could bear, and if an opportunity arose to escape after half an hour, then all the better.

My mind would wander as I sat there, and I would watch the other patients with a kind of fascination. They were all totally absorbed in their own worlds, with little or no communication to anyone. Who were all of these people, I wondered, and why were they all there? I often say, We wear our script on our face—that our faces tell our life stories—but everyone in "The Mental" had the same face.

Their pupils dilated from medications, they sat there with blank stares, utterly withdrawn from the world. It was such a surreal feeling to be in a room with people who were not present, and the saddest thing was the inevitability that some were going to be there year after year, caught up in the cycle but never making any real progress, and that group included my mother. Yet they could not be all crazy, I thought. There had to be something deeper going on.

My mother had gone to medical school, and she could regale us with the intricacies of how kidneys work, how they secrete the body's waste materials and then reabsorb the chemicals that keep the system in balance. I was always riveted by her accounts of the miraculous way the body functions.

And yet as I sat beside her in a psychiatric hospital, I was struck by the incredible complexity of the mind and the ways that we human beings are connected and attached to one another, and how little psychiatrists knew about what they were treating. I became fascinated by how little we knew about what was present, and wondered if one day it would be possible to know as much about brains, minds and love, as we do about the other systems that make up our organism. As a result, I set out from an early age to learn to navigate the human condition in a receivable format for wellness.

As soon as I turned eighteen, I left my house to join the army, really believing that I was leaving my past behind me and was going on to make a fresh start. But as I was to discover years later, the past, particularly if you have no awareness and understanding of your programming, is always with you in the present moment, and it can have a very negative effect on your present and future.

MY ARMY FAMILY

My first day in the army was fantastic. It was a wet autumn day. I left my house around 10 am to walk the five or six minutes up the road to the local barracks where my transport awaited me. There were no sad goodbyes. We were not that kind of family. I just put my bag on my shoulder and walked out the door. I felt a great sense of adventure that day, of something new and exciting. This was my ticket out of that house, and I would not have minded if I never went back inside those doors.

We arrived at the central training camp around midday, and it was bustling with activity. It felt huge—it was nearly like a small town in its own right. There were drills taking place on the square, there was shouting everywhere. My only thought was, *Wow*.

The jeep dropped us off at the recruiting office, and our platoon sergeant came out to greet us. I had expected the superior officer to scream and roar at us from the go, but he was pleasant and genial as he welcomed us to our new home. Then, after a murky lunch of something that they claimed was beef stew and which was memorable for all the wrong reasons, my group of recruits was taken to the quartermaster's store to be kitted out with our uniforms.

We were then taken to our billet, one in a series of red-bricked buildings that were once British army barracks and that would be home for the next six months.

Twelve of us were assigned to each billet, on six double bunks. The room was a high-ceilinged space with a pot-bellied stove in the middle for heat. The stove was turf fired, which meant that our duties would include morning trips to the nearby turf shed. But the whole space was pristine. I could even see my reflection on the green linoleum floor. The beds were supremely tidy, and each one came with a bed block: a stack of sheets and blankets folded into tight rectangles and arranged perfectly so that when the final blanket layered over the top sheet it fell within specified measurements. A good child's (like me) dream and nightmare.

We recruits spent the first evening in the billet introducing ourselves to one another, something I had never been good at. On the other hand, it was great: I was delighted to be in a place where nobody knew me or my family, and where I could be anonymous. But I was clearly a fish out of water. A lot of the others were tough, many of them from the inner cities, and some coming directly from state-run institutions. I was only one of a small number who had completed secondary-level education.

Waking up on that first morning, all I could think was, *Oh my God. Get me out of here.* Because then the shouting and roaring started. It was 6 am, to be exact, and the sergeant burst into the room at full volume, banging together two huge aluminum dustbin covers, and roaring at us to get out of bed. "I'm not your mother", he boomed. "Your mother is not going to help you now". A wake-up call in every sense of the word.

Oddly enough though, being the good child, I was used to the shouting and the drive for perfection, so I thrived in our tasks right from the start. I finally realized what my teachers had said: that I was intelligent, but previously had not been able to apply it.

I used that intelligent edge to my advantage over the coming months, and a lot of the recruits gravitated towards me if they were not sure of anything. I became the one all the guys came to if they had a letter with bad news from back home that they could either not read, or because they needed someone to share the bad news with. I was also fine-tuning the role of listener which I had learned from an early age. There were evenings I could sit around the pot-bellied stove in the billet, and guys, particularly the guys from the institutions and orphanages, would tell me their stories of growing up in such establishments.

I was always taken by people's willingness to tell me their deepest thoughts, knowing that they could trust me and that I was not going to be telling anybody else. It gave me great purpose and meaning to be able to provide such a role. So, in that sense my role of the good child was preferable to any of the other roles, if only I had known how to deal with my own deep-rooted anxiety and darkness.

Still though, it felt good to be needed, and it also felt good to know that I had a way to avoid being picked on, by being a valuable asset. But in the end, it was this defense that became my undoing, because while I thought I was diverting all the danger on the outside, on the inside the anxiety and darkness was growing. When you are the good child, the one people come to for help, you always have to be a step ahead. You have to be better and better, the best.

As paradoxical as it sounds, the relentless striving for perfection was actually worse for me now that I was succeeding in my assigned tasks. Whereas in school I was able to shuffle along with good but not remarkable grades, now I was out in front of the pack and feeling pressure to stay there. For this reason, and because I got good energy from the recognition and the sense of belonging that this role gave me, I constantly pushed myself to do more and more things well, feeling that my best was never good enough. Never mind that other people thought that I was cool and doing well—nothing I did was ever good enough for me.

After six months I graduated, and moved to another barracks. I went back to the Central Training Depot in 1979 to do my junior leader's course, and graduated after six months.

I married my childhood sweetheart, Mary, in 1982, and although on the surface that was a very happy time, I always lived with an almost constant sense of darkness and doom, that I had no language for. This mental state incrementally eats away at your whole sense of being. You cannot tell anyone, even those closest to you, because the truth is that you do not know what to tell people.

In April 1983 I embarked on a six-month overseas mission with the United Nations to the Middle East. Three months into that tour of duty, things had gotten so dark for me that I just wanted out.

Not necessarily out of the war zone, and not even necessarily out of life. I wanted to be out of the pain, out of the utterly repressive mission I had assigned to myself throughout my entire life: to be perfect. The perfect child, the perfect student, the perfect soldier, the perfect everything. It was exhausting, and I had had enough. I wanted to die, I wanted to end the constant torture in my soul, and I tried to die. I only survived due to the intervention and the presence of the chaplain of the forces, who unknowingly came across me in a very distressed state after a failed attempt to end my life.

When I came home from that overseas trip, I did not tell anybody what had happened out of fear of being judged (and being labelled mad like my mother). I did promise the chaplain, however, that I would go and speak to somebody, and he set me up for an appointment with a therapist. I went for several visits, but it never really clicked for me, as I felt the therapist talked too much and was not really listening to me.

Although my first tour of overseas service was a difficult personal experience, in hindsight there was a positive aspect to it as well, as I began to see the power of the human spirit in action. This was in the way the people of the villages who had experienced severe trauma through war and conflict could still come together in a very positive way for survival. As I witnessed more and more varied experiences and environments; I kept returning to the effects that different circumstances had on different people. I was fascinated by the fact that no matter how difficult the environment, people could manage to thrive; how was this?

When we returned from an overseas trip, we would get four weeks' leave. This in essence was a recovery period to allow us to ease our way back into normal life again. During that time, I began to question whether the army was really where I wanted to spend my career.

I signed up for a beginners' course in Psychology in a local college, and although I found it fascinating, in a slightly skewed way, the course did not teach me ways to treat or understand mental health that were any different than those that my mother would have been subjected to in "The Mental". On the contrary, it was largely concerned with theories and abstract thinking that had little practical use from what I could see. But in addition to piquing my interest in areas I became curious to know more about, it did give me an insight into the kinds of labelling and categorizing that I knew I wanted to avoid.

Late one Saturday night, and into the early hours of Sunday morning, a young soldier died by suicide in the army barracks.

This young soldier like myself had recently returned from overseas duty; in fact, he was in my platoon. I was devastated, not alone for the loss of such a young man who had huge potential, but why did I live and this lovely young man die? I became a man obsessed with trying to understand.

One day, a couple of months after this tragic incident, I had a call from my commanding officer, who wanted to see me in his office. At the meeting he told me that the army was very concerned about the recent number of suicides in the services, and were looking to set up some form of information, support and listening service for soldiers and their families. He was very keen to set up such a service in our own local barracks.

He felt that I possessed the qualities that would be necessary to provide such a service, and would I be interested? Of course, I was, and after a rigorous selection process I was dispatched for training. A number of months later I arrived back to set up the army's first personnel support service.

I found that I took to this work like a duck to water. I had always been known as a listener and somebody you could confide in, and this meant that increasing numbers of people came into my office when they had problems and needed a gentle listening ear. I found that I had a great empathy for other people's hurt and pain, and I also found that I was able to escape from my own darkness by hiding in another person's darkness. This made me very good at my job, and it also gave me a much clearer insight of where to begin my studies, so back I went to college.

My primary training was in Clinical Counselling and Psychotherapy. This was perfect in that it helped me to fine-tune my skills in listening, understanding, being non-judgmental and objective, and creating a safe space where people could feel comfortable telling their stories.

I felt it was a real privilege for any person to allow me into the darkness of their world. It is a privilege that should always be understood and respected.

The one thing that I found fascinating from early on was how much other people's stories mirrored my own story, and that in essence we were all merely characters in the same story of life. We all had one thing in common: the feeling of not belonging, and compensating in some way for that feeling of misplacement by constantly seeking approval and appreciation. I needed that bit of light that I got from helping others; it gave me a purpose. It allowed me to focus on something other than how broken I was inside.

I had so many dark thoughts and dark days, but I felt that if I could make a difference in someone's life in a real positive way, living with that darkness was worth it no matter what the price.

More and more the issues coming into the office were connected to overseas service, and the difficulties that soldiers and their families were experiencing. I became part of a pioneering group who were involved in setting up debriefing groups that looked at supporting and educating soldiers around trauma and critical incidents that they may have experienced on an overseas mission.

It was during my second critical incident debrief in the Middle East that I made an interesting discovery. I had come across a soldier who was involved on the periphery of a major incident, and who seemed to be struggling much more than the other soldiers involved. This soldier was traumatized, and when we sat down and chatted in a safe environment, I discovered that there was a very traumatic incident in his childhood about which he had never spoken.

The recent critical incident brought back all of his traumatic memories from childhood, and the latter was now overwhelming him. This was very relevant for me because of my childhood experience, and I was determined to learn a lot more. I dived headlong into my work with a great passion.

I became obsessed with my work. My work in trauma and the education of trauma took me all over the world, from the Middle East to the Balkan States, from East Timor to Africa. It was a great privilege to work with people in the darkest moments of their lives, in some of the darkest places on the planet. It gave me a great sense of belonging, of having a purpose. It allowed me to escape from that deep visceral pain that never let me go. I did not realize that in my yearning to belong, in my fear of being swallowed up by the past, I was really only pushing my hidden pain deeper inside of me.

I had not yet discovered that my silence and my desire for acceptance, both founded in fear, were both ways of running away from myself, and that in deciding not to face the past and myself directly, I was creating my own prison. I had my secret and my secret had me.

For much of my adult life I had thought that my survival in the present depended on keeping the past and its darkness locked away. I was a nine-year-old boy chasing the dream of making the world a better place, constantly seeking approval and appreciation, and learning to hide in other people's darkness to avoid my own darkness. I really wanted to know how a person survives and even thrives in the wake of trauma. How do people create lives of joy, purpose and passion, no matter what sorrows they have experienced?

I wanted to know how to meet everyday challenges and survive devastating experiences. How to live with our past and our mistakes, how people heal. What if my mother had someone to talk to; would she have had a happier life? Would we have had a happier life?

I became obsessed with education, knowledge, anything to help me understand and navigate the human condition. I studied psychology, neurology, biology, psychiatry, spirituality, genetics, neuroscience, epigenetics, quantum physics, and all the great philosophers.

I sought out workshops, study groups, and conferences that covered the work of a vast number of educators: from Descartes to Lamarck, Janet to Newton, Freud to Lipton, Bradshaw to Winnicott, Siegal to Pert, Van der Kolk to Ledoux, to name but a few.

I travelled all over the world to access these workshops and conferences. It was while I was in New York in 1997, attending one of these workshops on the work of Stephen Porges, that I became aware of a study regarding "Adverse Childhood Experiences (ACE)". This was ongoing research that looked at the "relationship of childhood abuse and household dysfunction to many of the leading causes of deaths in adults".

I dived headfirst into researching this study and trying to find out everything I could about it for two reasons. Firstly, in my own work as a therapist and working with soldiers in traumatic incidents, it was interesting to see how many of them who had psychological or physical illnesses as adults had also had childhood traumatic experiences. Secondly, I became really concerned about myself; was I going to get sick? I became so anxious and preoccupied with trying to find out answers that it took over my life. I lived in fear of getting sick and dying.

I borrowed heavily to meet my research commitments. I got into severe financial debt. I remortgaged the house. I was dishonest, I hurt people. I hid everything. In hindsight. My actions and behaviors became more impulsive and irrational, sometimes bordering on reckless.

My attic was full of boxes with reams and reams of notes and workshop materials. I was trying to put together a massive tapestry, a way of understanding, trying to see the data and the connections all at once, and trying to spot the unseen ties that would lead me to a greater understanding of the human condition.

I would often sleep with the data under my bed, as if the data would sift up into my mind and reveal the answers in my dreams.

MY FAMILY

Nobody knew of the tortured world that I lived in, not even my family. I had perfected the persona of the good child, the fixer, to placate, to keep people happy. It is very hard to describe this to people. How could one acquire so much knowledge and education and yet live a life of such secrecy? There is no easy answer to this question.

I know now from reading Paddy Rafter's website and story that it was because I had no awareness of myself. It was my faulty childhood programming. I also now know that the human condition will do anything to survive and protect itself. Personas such as mine become real to a person and are a way of surviving, but they are also a way of avoiding the judgement and the shame that will inevitably come from people. It is a bit like being caught in a spider's web; the more you try to get free, the more you get trapped.

As earlier mentioned, I married my childhood sweetheart Mary in 1982. Our plan was to wait a year or two before having children in order to give us a chance to settle into married life and to make the house more suitable for a family, but then, when we started trying to have children, we had no luck.

A year passed, and another, and another, in which we underwent physical and psychological testing to see what the problem might be—a compassionless, humiliating process that only fed my innate sense of not being good enough. (How could I fail at that most basic act of becoming a father? Could I not even get that right?)

My fear of intimacy was crippling, and I was so alone in my darkest thoughts. I felt I was in some way being punished by God for what had happened to me as a child.

We knew we had other options though, so after four or five years we decided to pursue the route of adoption. It was during this adoption process that Mary became pregnant, and nine months later Joseph was born. Nearly three years later Jenny was born.

You might dare to say it was nearly perfect—except that was how I tried to force it to be. Of course, there were happy times, but there was also the anxiety that I introduced into the mix so incrementally that I didn't even notice for years afterwards. It was the little things, and they all started to add up. Everything had to be perfect, and everything had to be on time. I could never trust that everything was going to be okay; there was always that deep-down feeling of impending disaster and doom. If we were going to the seaside on a Sunday, I had it in my head that we had to leave at 10 am sharp.

But what family with young children ever leaves at any time sharp? So, by five or ten minutes past the hour, my anxiety would kick in. We would then end up bickering the whole way there and there would be tears in the back seat while poor Mary felt the pressure in the passenger seat. I had grown up in an environment where I learned to expect that things would always go wrong, so I was still expecting the same result—which is a perfect way to cause that very result, as it turns out. The more perfect I tried to make things, the more imperfect they became.

The result of this, of course, is that having grown up in a really anxious environment, through my own anxiety, I was unknowingly creating the same anxious environment in my own family. It is a bit like the whole spider web analogy again; the more you try to escape it and change it, the more trapped in it you become.

Joseph's mental health in particular suffered because of this anxious environment, and he had a real battle with his mental health all through his childhood, adolescence and young adult years which culminated in hospitalizations and attempts at suicide. I of course blamed myself, which I know sounds narcissistic, but I genuinely believed that in some way I was to blame for all of his difficulties. This only added to my deep sense of guilt, inadequacy and imperfection.

After a number of years things began to settle down for Joseph, and although that was good, the constant fear and the irrational feeling of impending disaster which I carried deep down within me all my life never left me.

My way of coping with that fear and darkness was to go find somebody to help. By this time my work had almost totally evolved into doing talks and presentations using my lifelong experience of trauma, anxiety, and mental health in families.

I was busy going all over the country (and outside), standing on stages telling our family story, and it really brought it home to me the thousands and thousands of families all over the place who were struggling with the exact same issues we struggled with as a family. All that was really happening was that while standing on stage, I was just connecting to people with similar experiences, and it had the effect of normalizing all of our experiences. My presentations became hugely popular. I was speaking at venues all over the country, from theatres to hotels, to school halls, to country halls with sometimes five or six hundred people or more in attendance.

One thing that my childhood experiences gave me was an ability to empathize with people, and in a way almost reach into their souls and feel their hurt and pain. This worked really well for me as it helped me to cope with my own almost constant sense of fear and darkness. As I became massively popular and in demand as a speaker, my working day was increasing to twelve, fourteen, sometimes sixteen hours.

In a sense I was living the dream, a dream of a nine-year-old hurt boy who wanted to grow up and make a difference in the world in a positive way. You would have thought that I would be happy and content, but the opposite was the reality.

I was leaving my house early in the morning, driving three hours, delivering presentations, getting back into the car, driving for another two hours, presenting again. Going to bed in a hotel (not sleeping) as I constantly played presentations over and over in my head and worried that people would not like me. Getting up again at 6 am and driving for another three hours. This was going on for six, sometimes seven days a week. I would not say no to anybody (the good child) from a deep-rooted fear that others would not like me. I could get a standing ovation on nights from five hundred people, and twenty-five minutes later I would be pulled in at the side of the road in a totally dark and desperate place, in floods of tears and not knowing why.

I did the only thing that I knew from childhood; I pretended that everything was okay (when it clearly was not). I took on more presentations, full of the fear of saying no.

My family was noticing and tried to talk to me, because I was on a fast track to burn out. Imagine being on a roller coaster and you can't get off. But really you don't want it to stop, because it is the only thing that is allowing you to survive, and you are terrified that if it stops that you will be totally enveloped in darkness.

A short while later I was doing presentations in a nearby city for the day. I had taken the early morning train, and on arriving at the main train station I took a tram to continue to my destination. The tram was very crowded and I just about got a seat. At the next stop a very elderly obese man got on and squeezed into the seat beside me. I did not know why at that time, but I experienced a massive panic attack. I thought I would never get to the next stop. I managed to get off at the next stop, sat down at the curb and used my breathing to ground myself. After about five minutes I settled and decided to walk the rest of the journey to where I was presenting. It had been many years since I had a panic attack of this nature, and I really was not sure why, but I did what I always do, I focused on my work.

By the time that I got back home that evening I was exhausted and was in bed early. That night, for the first time in a long time, I had extreme nightmares and night tremors. These nightmares went on for some weeks. I was screaming and shouting in my sleep and pleading for somebody to mind me. I would cry constantly in my sleep. I remember very little other than waking up with a feeling of absolute terror. My wife was deeply concerned as it was waking her up and she did not know what to do.

The nightmares began to settle down around Christmas time but came back again with a vengeance in February. At this point they became so frightening that I would not sleep at all, and I would lie there all night forcing my eyes to stay open rather than close them and risk descending into the terror and the darkness. At this point I was not sleeping, I was struggling to eat, and I was working flat out, which was the only way I knew to keep the darkness at bay. You would have thought that with all my years of knowledge and experience that I would have talked to somebody and tried to do something about it.

But unfortunately, that is not the way it works, because (as I discovered afterwards) I was so far into the survival brain that my logical and rational brain had almost disappeared.

I was heading very quickly into burnout. On a Monday night in late March the nightmare was so intense that I thought I was going to suffocate. There was this great big fireball coming right at me, and I had no way of stopping it. I was terrified, and as the fireball came nearer to my face, a vision began to materialize in the fireball. It was somebody I had hidden in the deepest recesses of my mind for nearly fifty years, my childhood abuser. I woke up in a lather of sweat, screaming. I will never forget the terror of that moment. But did I tell anyone? No. Why?

Because I thought that I could push it back down, and I did not want my family to see me as some dirty little abused child.

The next couple of days were all about trying to survive. I did not know then that I had descended into a very dark and very dangerous psychiatric space. I did not know until much later that what had happened on the tram the previous November was that the very strong smell of body odor from the elderly man who had sat so close to me, had triggered deeply repressed memories of my own childhood abuser and brought on a panic attack. The waves of emotions that were now enveloping me were terrifying, and the impulses to do something to myself were frightening.

A couple of mornings later I left my house to die. The only way I could describe it was that it was almost like being in a trance. I had left behind details for my funeral, including choices of songs and singers. I knew where I was going to die and what I was going to do.

When I arrived at my destination, I got out of the car and sat at the side of the river. I don't know why, but I became engulfed in floods of tears. For some reason my deceased mother's face came into my head.

My mother spent most of her life wanting to die, but she ultimately lived until she was eighty-six. I thought of my wife and family, and the fact that we had been through so much as a family and had survived.

I do not know what spirit guided my hand to take my phone and ring my son, but I did. I asked him if he could go and get his mother and his sister and bring them to our house and wait for me there. When I arrived home, they were sitting in the living room.

We all sat down and I told them what was happening to me. Telling them about my abuse was the single most difficult thing I have ever had to do in my entire life. They only ever knew me as this strong husband and father who tried to go out and help people all his life; was this going to color how they saw me? I told them about my desire to die. At this point I was in a deep state of trauma.

They called my GP, who when he saw me arranged for an immediate admission to a psychiatric hospital as (in his opinion) I had become extremely psychiatrically unwell.

This hospital became my home for the next eight weeks, and I was diagnosed with Post Traumatic Stress Disorder dating back to childhood sexual abuse.

My first morning waking up in hospital I could only describe as the lowest feeling I have ever experienced. The sense of defeat, of loneliness, of hopelessness was paralyzing. It was almost as if my greatest fears and nightmares had all come true at the one time. My greatest fear had been that I would end up like my mother, and yet here I was.

I remember meeting the consultant psychiatrist who was to look after me. I bawled and cried incoherently, pleading with him not to electrocute me and fill me with tablets (like my mother); the fear of this happening was crippling. He was a kind, soft-spoken man who just listened to me, and assured me that this would not be the case and that I would fully be a part of my treatment plan.

I genuinely believe, looking back at that morning now, that the dignity and the respect that this young consultant afforded me in that initial interview was the key that allowed me over time to confront my fears and hurts of over fifty years.

The first visit of Mary, Joseph and Jenny to the hospital five days later was horrific for me. Although I was delighted to see them, the shame and humiliation that I felt was something I will never forget. I was supposed to be the strong one, the one who fixed things for everyone else, and here I was completely helpless and in a deep state of hopelessness. I did not want to see the pity in their eyes. Their big strong father was reduced to this. But there was a great strength in the four of us being together, and that strength of family love offered some hope.

One morning early on in my hospital stay one of the residents in my unit was going home for good, having finished his treatment. We had been chatting at breakfast, and I asked him if he had any tips to help me survive my time in the unit. He looked at me intently and said, "Just be honest with yourself". It was probably the most powerful but also the most challenging advice that I ever had received. But I was willing to take it on board and do whatever it took to get well.

Sitting down in therapy rooms was a bit like someone putting a mirror in front of you and asking you to look at yourself as you really are.

It was painful, full of hurt and anger, shameful, and humiliating; but mixed in with all of these emotions was a tiny seed beginning to grow, a growing sense of freedom, in that although the memories were painful, that's all they were—memories, and they could not hurt me anymore.

I began to learn that I was obsessed with trying to be someone, with earning my place in the world. I had created my own prison, telling myself that no matter what I did, I would never be good enough. I had spent my life trying to make a difference and trying to understand.

I wanted to be someone who fit in, who wasn't plagued by the idea of being different, or being cursed, or playing catch up forever in a relentless race away from the darkness of the past. I lived my life in fear, and nobody would ever have known.

Fear is a killer; if you succumb to it, it saps your energy and keeps you from thinking straight. You are afraid of the past, and of the future, and the present is so dark that you get lost in it and almost become the darkness. I didn't know that fears kept hidden only became fiercer. I didn't know that my habits of placating and pleasing were only making me worse.

My time in the hospital helped me to realize how precious life is, and how fragile. Too short, life is too short to settle for anything less than the love, compassion and empathy which we are all capable of giving and receiving.

Coming back home into the real world and away from the cocoon of the hospital was very difficult. I could not deal with the deep sense of shame and humiliation. I was this fragile child who had spent a lifetime placating and pleasing and trying to make a difference in the world, just to survive the deep-rooted feelings of fear and inadequacy.

I didn't know what to do. I descended into a deep dark state of depression, and I could not leave the house. Some of the time I could not leave my bedroom. I was paralyzed with fear, and that fear was having a massive negative impact on almost every aspect of my life. I had learned, by experience this time, that this is trauma: a nearly constant feeling in my gut that something is wrong or that something terrible is going to happen. The automatic fear responses in my body telling me to run away, to take cover, to hide myself from the danger that is everywhere.

Every part of me wanted to die. There were days when it would have been easier to die than to live; it was like death by a thousand cuts. Normally, over the years when I experienced something like this, I just poured myself into my work and kept myself busy, kept running. But now I had no place to run to, I was too unwell, I just had to sit in the terror.

I was in an awful hole of darkness. It almost felt as if my entire life had been one great big lie. Despite all my counselling background and training. Despite my almost-obsessive journeys all over the world to listen to the most up-to-date, cutting-edge speakers in science and psychology. Despite having experience at working with trauma in the most unique frontline locations of war and conflict and the great understanding that that afforded me. Ultimately, I felt a complete failure, as none of these things brought healing and peace to my own life.

How could I know so much and yet know so little?

I was riddled with guilt and an ever-increasing sense of fear and hopelessness. I felt like a complete fraud and perceived that this was the way everybody saw me.

One evening, by providence, a friend of mine brought me to an open meeting of the AA fellowship. The guest speaker on this particular evening was Paddy Rafter.

Some of the things that Paddy spoke about I didn't quite understand at that time, as I had never heard those things spoken about in that way before. However, I heard enough to realize that some chord had been struck deep inside of me, and I wanted to hear more from this man. As I was at such a low point, I reached out and made arrangements to meet up with Paddy to talk.

Through fortuitous circumstances I was able to meet Paddy a good number of times. Over that period of time, I began to understand what he was saying about the true reality of life and suffering. He shared with me his story as he had done with many others.

I became an avid and ardent follower, almost like a disciple. I met Paddy on a one-to-one basis on many occasions over the next couple of years. His teaching and sharing of the 48 Acts changed my whole life. It made a major positive impact on me in a real, coherent, whole and natural way. I learned to accept myself as I truly was for the very first time. It gave me intimations beyond understanding.

The strangest thing was that it gave me a new understanding of my work in counselling and trauma and the thinking and the science behind it. My understanding of the science of counselling changed profoundly.

Therefore, I am trying to approach this book from a couple of unique perspectives:

Firstly, from the way his teachings of the 48 Acts affected me from both a personal and a professional counselling/science perspective.

Secondly, how his teachings allowed me to understand all the counselling and science I would have cognitively learned over my entire working life; they gave me a different perspective of gut and instinctual knowledge that was to have a profound positive impact on my journey to recovery.

Therefore, I resolved to do this layman's guide from my uniquely personal perspective of hearing and working with Paddy in person as he expounded his ideas over a number of years.

Furthermore, I wish to incorporate my understanding of the modern, counselling-based thinking behind these Acts, and reflect the transformation in my perspective in a way that can be read by anyone.

Fundamentally, I am an eyewitness.

Fundamentally, I am the first disciple.

I will take you through my understanding of how each Act led me on a path to recovery that was ultimately

Real
Coherent

Whole and natural.

But before I do that, I will give a new perspective about my understanding of the science behind all of this, which I hope will be of help to anybody seeking a different way of "knowing". Reading and absorbing this upcoming section are of the utmost importance as it gives a very detailed scientific understanding of why anxiety is the cause of ninety five percent of the mind and the body becoming sick and in lots of cases death. This new understanding was to save my life, and allow me to become well, and will do the same for you.

I would never have realized that I was an anxious person, and yet for almost my entire life my entire being was permeated with anxiety and fears almost to the point of death.

I always thought that my problems were outside of my control and that there was nothing I could do about them anyway.

What I never realized until I became intimately involved with Paddy Rafter's *48 Acts Towards a New Way of Living* was how my thoughts and perceptions were having such a negative impact on my life and were only increasing my fears and anxieties.

This was despite over thirty years of study and practice as a counsellor in which I had assiduously studied all the current thinking on the topic. Indeed, I had gone so far as to fly all over the world to attend lectures and study days with some of the leading experts who also worked at the coalface and the intersection between mental health and wellness. I learned a tremendous amount from those experts and the ideas they espoused, and even assimilated them into my work. Yet, despite all this I was still lost.

Fear was just like the bogeyman to me, always in the background waiting to get me, and I was compensating in many different ways to stay ahead of him. I began to get well only when I began to understand, in a different way, words such as "fear", "anxiety", "thoughts", "perceptions", "programming", and "addiction to approval and appreciation".

I will explain perception in a different way as I go along, but to me it was thinking almost all the time that everything was not going to be okay, and always waiting for something to go wrong.

Even when everything was going okay, I could not trust that it was going to stay okay, because my thinking told me differently. So here is the question:

How does the nature of our perceptions, influence what happens in our lives?

In order to become well, I discovered that it was of vital importance to have some form of workingman's knowledge of how the mind, brain and body work together, but I did not need to be an expert. For me, I just needed to understand how my life had gotten into such difficulty.

While growing up, and also in my later life, there were a lot of difficulties and a history of addiction, depression, sexual abuse, loneliness, isolation, and suicidal intentions. I have been hurt in my life, but I have also hurt other people. I have made mistakes that have impacted the lives of others. I have done things that I am not proud of.

However, I have discovered, through a developing understanding of the 48 Acts, that in order to break free of the chains that always held me back, I needed to become more aware and learn to live in the reality of the present moment, no matter how painful it may feel. There are times when reality is not a nice place to be (which is why I spent a lifetime trying to escape it) because it means looking at my own reflection in the mirror, and learning to take personal responsibility for my own thoughts, words, actions, and behaviors.

Reality in the short term is not pleasant, but in the long term it is life-changing, life-affirming, and hugely nurturing.

From this program I learned that the only way to awareness is through knowledge and understanding. Sourcing and implementing the upcoming knowledge and understanding, and connecting it to my own life story, was a contributing factor in coming into recovery, as it is based in absolute reality.

Danger and fear are a normal part of life and have been since humans first came on the planet, which means that sometimes we have to make the journey backwards before we can move forward in harmony with ourselves and the world around us. So, let your mind go back in time to when we were hunter-gatherers living in our clans and tribes on the savannas, totally in touch with nature and where we had a great sense of belonging.

On a particular day, two of our ancestors were out hunting for food on the savanna. Suddenly, a twig snapped, a giant saber-toothed tiger appeared in front of them, gobbled up one of them, and the other one ran away as quick as he could back to the safety of the tribe.

The following day our lone ancestor was out hunting on his own, because in those days if you did not hunt, you did not eat.

He happened to end up in the same area of the savanna as the previous day, and all of a sudden, a twig snapped behind him.

What do you think he did? You got it, he ran. Why did he run? Because something told him that the last time he heard a twig snap, a saber-toothed tiger appeared and gobbled up his colleague. So, instinctively he ran.

What was the difference between the first day and the second day?

The first day's reaction was based on a REALITY. He actually saw the tiger, and ran for survival based on the reality of the tiger standing right in front of him.

The second day's reaction was based on a PERCEPTION. He never actually saw the tiger. He reacted to the SOUND of a twig snapping and assumed it was a tiger. In actual fact, if he had paused for a moment and taken a deep breath, he would have discovered it was a rabbit which he could have had for lunch; but equally, his perception could have been right and he would have been a meal himself.

So, what is a perception?

A perception is the ability to see, hear, or become aware of something through the five senses: SOUND, SIGHT, SMELL, TASTE, and TOUCH. But you must understand this. Perception is our interpretation of the sound, sight, smell, taste, or touch as it pertains to us and our previous experiences.

Fundamentally, perception is a survival tool developed millions of years ago. Perception is not reality, but for most people living in the modern postindustrial world, their perceptions have become their reality. Without awareness, this is having massive negative implications for the well-being of individuals, society and the world in general.

The truth is that our brain does not know the difference between perception and reality. We actually have to tell it.

What I am going to do here is take you through my understanding of science. My understanding of the science I had previously learned deepened immensely because of the new perspective that I received from my total immersion and interaction with the 48 Acts. Ultimately, by understanding it in this way and using different visualization's of what was going on in my head and my body, I became well. I cannot emphasize enough how important understanding it in this way was for me, because once I understood how everything worked and could piece it all together, I felt really empowered. Guess what? **You can deal with what you know,** but **you cannot deal with what you do not know.** It deals with you.

What we are really talking about here of course is our MIND. The problem though is that we have two minds. If we just had one mind, life would be so much simpler. Did you ever make your mind up to do something, but there was another voice going on in your head doubting you and telling you something different?

I am going to explain to you why we have two minds and what function they serve, and ultimately break it down into a simpler language which will make it easier to understand.

OUR BRAIN

Matthew Cobb's definitive book *The Idea of the Brain* tells "the story of centuries of discovery, showing how brilliant minds, some of them now forgotten, first identified that the brain is the organ that produces thought and then began to show what it might be doing, but despite a solid bedrock of understanding, the four most important words in the science of understanding the brain are 'We do not know'." With that in mind, I set about understanding all I could about what science does know about the brain.

The most important task of the brain is to ensure our survival.

To accomplish this the brain needs to:

Generate internal cues that indicate what our body needs,

Draw a map of the world to assist us on our journey to ameliorate these needs,

Create the energetic responses required to get us there,

point out the danger along the way, and coordinate the responses.

Physical, emotional and mental problems occur when our internal cues become unbalanced.

The brain evolved over the course of our evolution and was built in three tiers from the bottom up.

THE FIRST TIER

This is the oldest part of the brain and the part that is online when we are born. It is called the ancient animal brain. It is located in the brain stem just above where the spinal cord enters the skull. It is responsible for all the things that newborn babies can do, like eat, sleep, breathe, cry, etc.

THE SECOND TIER

The second part of the brain to evolve was the limbic system. This is also known as the mammalian brain, and it sits right above the ancient animal brain. Development of the limbic system takes off right after a baby is born. It is sometimes called the emotional brain as it is the seat of the emotions. It is the detector of danger and the adjudicator of what is important for survival purposes.

Taken together, the limbic system and the ancient animal brain make up what I call the survival brain. The survival brain's main task is to look out for our welfare, safety and survival. The survival brain is like a long-term memory; it remembers everything for our survival. It is our unconscious/subconscious mind. It is not something to be afraid of.

In reality, the subconscious is just an emotionless database of stored programs whose job specification is strictly concerned with reading signals from the environment and activating automated, hard-wired behavioral responses. It has no discernment and asks no questions. It is a bit like a programmed hard drive into which our life experiences are downloaded.

It stores our belief systems (which in our earlier years were programmed in for us by somebody else). The roles we learned in childhood. All our unexpressed emotions. It even remembers the little girl who called you rude names in second grade. It might not remember her name, but it sure remembered and stored the memory of how you felt at that time.

This is mind number one. Emotional brain, survival brain, subconscious mind. It is the part that evolved first. This is the part that doubts you, questions you, chatters away to you (never with good news, funnily enough). So, when you are anxious, hurt, angry, acting out, shamed, guilty, etc., this is the part of your head that you are in. For my own simplified way of understanding this, I call this mind the RED ZONE, and if you get stuck in this area, life will not be good.

So, where is our other mind?

THE THIRD TIER

Our other mind is the newest part of the brain, namely the neocortex (our rational or conscious mind), and this is where the brain reached its present size and structure with a full expansion of the frontal lobes.

This is the part of the brain that makes us uniquely smart compared to other living organisms; once again for my own simplification I call this mind the BLUE ZONE. This is the youngest part of the brain.

The Blue Zone is primarily concerned with the world outside of us, understanding how things and people work, and figuring out how to accomplish our goals, manage our time, and sequence our actions.

The Blue Zone enables us to use language and abstract thought; it gives us our ability to absorb and integrate vast amounts of information and attach meaning to it.

The Blue Zone allows us to plan and reflect, to imagine and play out future scenarios. It makes choices possible and underlies our astonishing creativity.

The Blue Zone is the one that says "I would love to do a bungee jump"; the Red Zone is the one that immediately says "Oh no you won't", and the battle of minds and words continues.

I found this idea of the Red Zone/Blue Zone very helpful on my journey to recovery as it allowed me to visualize what was actually going on in my head. I learned that if I could balance the two, I could become very well, but if they went out of balance, I could become very unwell.

So, what makes them go out of balance?

FEAR AND ANXIETY.

To understand all of this in greater detail, let us go back and look at what happened to our ancestor on the second day.

As I said earlier, danger is a normal part of life, and the brain is in charge of detecting it and organizing our response. Sensory information about the outside world arrives through our five senses.

In our ancestors' case the sound of the twig snapping was picked up in the Red Zone by the thalamus (which is observing the environment all the time for danger using our five senses).

This sensation picked up by the thalamus is automatically sent in two directions: down to the amygdala, two small, almond-shaped structures that lie deeper in the Red Zone and up to the frontal lobes, where they reach our Blue Zone.

The American neuroscientist Joseph Le Doux calls the pathway to the amygdala the "low road", which is extremely fast, and the pathway to the frontal lobes the "high road", which takes several milliseconds longer in the midst of a perceived overwhelmingly threatening experience. This of course means that the amygdala receives the message first.

The central function of the amygdala is to decide whether incoming input is pertinent to our survival.

It does so quickly and automatically, with the help of feedback from the hippocampus, a nearby structure that relates new input to past experiences.

So, what is the past experience stored in our ancestors' hippocampus?

"Oh my God there is a tiger behind me, because the last time I heard the sound of a twig snap, a tiger appeared and gobbled up my colleague, I need to get out of here".

Armed with this backup information from the hippocampus, the amygdala sends an instant message down to the hypothalamus and the brain stem, calling into play the stress hormone system and the autonomic nervous system to notify the cells and orchestrate a whole-body response.

Because the Red Zone processes the information it receives quicker than the Blue Zone it decides whether incoming information is a threat to our survival even before we are consciously aware of the danger. By the time we become consciously aware of what is happening (if at all) our body may already be on the move.

WHAT HAPPENS NEXT?

Let us go back to our ancestor on the savanna when the twig has snapped on the second day, and the survival brain has sent a message that there is imminent danger and that the body must respond in kind.

Our mind represents a ruling body that coordinates the function of the body's massive cellular civilization. Our mind shapes the character of our cellular community

The mind and body are linked by a single regulatory system. These are a product of the simultaneous action between the two branches of the autonomic nervous system, the sympathetic, which acts as the body's "petrol pump", and the parasympathetic, which serves as its "brake".

These are the "reciprocals" Darwin spoke of, and working together they play off each other for preservation.

The sympathetic nervous system is responsible for arousal, including the fight, flight or freeze response (Darwin's "escape or avoidance behavior"). The sns moves blood to the muscles for quick action, partly by triggering the adrenal glands to release adrenaline, which speeds up the heart rate and increases blood pressure.

The second branch of the ANS is the parasympathetic nervous

system (PNS) which promotes self-protection functions like digestion and wound healing. It triggers the release of acetylcholine to put a break on arousal. Slowing the heart down, relaxing muscles, and returning breathing to normal.

How does all of this work?

Let us go back to our ancestors on the savanna.

The alarm has gone off (the twig has snapped). The signal has been received from our external environment

The message of impending danger has been sent down the brain stem to inform the cells.

"The membrane or skin of the cell is also the brain of the cell. Built into the membrane are protein switches that respond to the environmental signals by relaying their information to internal protein pathways. There are two protein switches, a receptor protein and an effector protein.

The receptor protein receives or senses signals from the environment. It then passes on the information to the effector protein. This connection then allows information from outside the cell to be transmitted into the cell where it is used to engage behavior. When activated by a receptor, the effector protein sends a secondary signal through a cytoplasm inside of the cell that controls specific protein functions and pathways.

Proteins are molecules in the cells, and they are like building blocks that come together to generate the cells behavior and function. Assemblies of proteins that provide specific biological functions are called pathways.

Receptor proteins provide the cell with an awareness of the signals being received from the environment. The effector proteins generate signals that regulate specific cell function".

It is important to remember that cells, tissues, and organs do not question information sent by the autonomic nervous system. Rather, they respond with equal intensity to accurate life-affirming perceptions (first day, when the tiger was standing right in front of our ancestor), and to self-destructive misperceptions (second day, when our ancestor reacted to the sound of a twig snapping).

"Our health is predicted by the nervous system's ability to accurately perceive environmental information and selectively engage appropriate, life-sustaining behaviors. If a mind misinterprets environmental signals and generates an inappropriate response, survival is threatened because the body's behaviors become out of synch with the environment."

As a way of understanding my own trauma and story of life, I began to visualize how all of this complex mixture of biology, neurology and physiology was playing out, in a more simple, understandable and practical way that worked for me.

I learned to break down the human organism at a physical level into three separate compartments for simplicity's sake.

At the center of the human organism is the visceral block or trunk: our abdomen, our chest, and the bits under our neck and above our hips, without the arms. The visceral block contains most of our systems. Our immune system, our digestive system, our endocrine system, our respiratory system, our reproductive system— nearly all our organs, our gut, our soul. This is where we were created and from where we were born. All human life was created in the visceral block.

The second block is your reflex block. This contains our musculoskeletal system, and it also contains the biggest organ in the human organism, our skin.

The third block is what I call the command center. This is the area above the neck, including brain and mind.

To see how all of this works in practice, let us go back to our ancestor when the twig snapped on the second day.

The message of danger from the command center is sent via the autonomic nervous system to our entire cellular community.

All the protein pathways are activated.

The increased pumping of the heart sends extra blood from the visceral block to the reflex block. This brings extra nutrition and oxygen to the muscles.

Muscle tension prepares for "fight, flight or freeze" defense.

Shortage of breath reduces rapid breathing, hyper-oxygenating the blood.

Sweating cools the body in anticipation of flight.

Greater production of blood glucose also helps bring more nutrition to the reflex block.

Secretion of adrenaline into the blood makes it clot easier should injury occur.

Blood circulation shifts from the digestive system to the muscles, leaving a cold empty feeling in the pit of the stomach and a tense readiness in the muscles.

A lot of systems in the visceral block become compromised as extra blood and oxygen are needed by the reflex block for survival; but that is okay, why?

Because when we were running from a tiger we were not going to be stopping to go to the bathroom, so it was okay to temporarily shut down these areas, or at least reduce their capacity in the short term.

It was appropriate to shut down our reproductive system; we most definitely were not going to be having sex while running from a tiger.

It was appropriate to shut down our digestive system, as we were not going to be sitting down to have a meal while we were running from or fighting a tiger. The blood was needed in the reflex block during the emergency.

As you can see, during the perceived emergency the visceral block learns to underperform, while the reflex block learns to overperform in the short term in order to ensure long-term survival. When the danger has passed, the whole organism comes back into balance.

The whole process is primarily a short-term response for survival and was never intended to be a long-term response. It sets up an endless loop of bodily hormones, gene expression and chemicals.

WHAT IS GOING ON IN YOUR HEAD ("COMMAND CENTRE") AT THIS TIME?

Neuroscience tells us that the contents of our head are eighty-six billion neurons, each one linked to ten thousand others, yielding trillions of connections.

A neuron communicates with its neighbor by converting the electrical signal from the environment into a chemical signal, a neurotransmitter, which then passes along the gap between the neurons (synapse) to bind to a receptor in the neighboring neuron, before being converted back into an electrical signal.

The three chemicals created and lumped together as stress hormones are adrenaline (epinephrine), noradrenaline (norepinephrine), and cortisol.

Adrenaline is the "fight or flight" hormone and is a product of the adrenal glands. Its effects are both immediate and short-acting.

Noradrenaline is the arousal hormone and a cousin of adrenaline. This is also fast-acting and makes us both hyper-alert and vigilant. Noradrenaline is secreted by both the adrenals and the brain, and it lasts longer than adrenaline.

Cortisol is the real survival hormone. The production of cortisol is a multistep approach which sets and brings into play all the key receptors like the adrenal gland, the hypothalamus, and the pituitary gland, which is also known as the HPA Axis.

Cortisol reduces levels of serotonin, dopamine, and gamma-aminobutyric acid (a calming neurotransmitter), which ends up causing mental health problems.

While in the "fight, flight or freeze" survival response, blood and oxygen will be directed mainly to the Red Zone as that is where the signal arrives first. It is important to remember that these emotional/biological responses far preceded the development of the Blue Zone so it makes sense that during prolonged periods of fear and perceived threats, a person would regress to the Red Zone for exactly that purpose, SURVIVAL.

One really important thing to remember is that all the above is happening literally within a nanosecond, automatically, linked to our thinking, and that is the way it has to be for survival. That is why we did survive and evolve, as we had an inbuilt system activated by INSTINCT to help us. So that response system in BALANCE is our friend, and it is there to help us.

IT IS NOT OUR FRIEND ANYMORE. WHY HAS IT BECOME OUR ENEMY?

I did not realize that within my troubled, traumatic life story, this system had become unbalanced within me. These out-of-balance programs and my lack of awareness of them were contributing factors in my maladaptive behaviors and responses, which caused havoc in my life and subsequently impacted the lives of others in my immediate environments.

I discovered through the 48 Acts that the only way I was going to become well was to gain a more holistic understanding of the consequences of not having awareness of my own personal story, and how that lack of awareness was giving me such a distorted view of both myself and the world around me.

UNDERSTANDING

For me, my progress has really been measured by understanding the work of Paddy Rafter and his 48 Acts, and trying to bring a new personal understanding of myself and my difficulties. So, in many ways it is about having a new understanding of what has gone before.

It is important to be aware that back in the earlier times of our evolution, language (as we know it) had not evolved. Language is only a recent part of our evolution.

I began to experience language in a more sensory and experiential way rather than cognitively, which was the only way I knew heretofore. This in turn began to give me a different meaning and understanding of my own narrative.

With this in mind I am going to bring you right back to the savanna and look at my changed understanding of what was happening.

Day one was based on REALITY: both heard the twig snap; both saw the tiger.

Day two was based on PERCEPTION, because our ancestor never actually saw the tiger. This was because when the twig snapped (and let us recap here):

The thalamus, which is a sensor in the Red Zone, picked up the sound of the twig snapping.

It immediately went on the alert, sensing "something is not right here".

The message was sent to the amygdala, whose function is to identify whether an incoming input is a threat to our survival. It does so quickly and unconsciously, with the help of feedback from the nearby hippocampus, which relates new input to past experiences.

The hippocampus remembered the experience of the day before when the twig snapped and went, "Oh my God, twig snapping means tiger coming" (it does not process, it just reacts automatically to the stimuli of the memory of the past experience) "we have to get this guy out of here immediately".

The message was passed on to the hypothalamus, which sent the message down the brain stem, which put the entire human organism into survival mode to deal with the incoming "perceived threat".

IN A MORE LAYMAN'S LANGUAGE

The minute you experience that instinctive sensation that everything is not okay or is not going to be okay, you are now evolving into the FEAR response system in the human organism.

By trying to understand my own story in the context of our evolution, I worked out that FEAR is something that back in hunter-gatherer times was our friend. It was an instinctive part of our evolution that was essential to our survival. We did not live in FEAR all the time. Most of the time we were in harmony with nature and our surroundings. We had a powerful sense of belonging within our clan and our tribe. We instinctively knew that in moments of crisis we had an inbuilt, instinctive survival mechanism (FEAR) in our Red Zone, and we trusted that in times of crisis that we would be okay. This is not to say that we lived in a utopian world, for we did not. But we did trust in nature and its surroundings.

FEAR is all about survival and it instantly creates an EMOTION.

In my efforts to impart some of my understanding of how I came into recovery within the 48 Acts, I am going to spend a little time here to look at three words, and how a changed understanding of these words set me on a path to wellness.

These three words are:

ENERGY
EMOTIONS
MOOD

Let us firstly look at ENERGY.

It was Einstein who implied, with his famous equation E = MC x 2, that everything in the world, from the physical, to the animal, to the human, is just ENERGY, and that everything is intertwined in ENERGY.

That is all we are, ENERGY.

When we were born and we took our first breath, all that happened was that through respiration, oxygen was metabolized to create ENERGY. In the same way, when we eat, the food we eat is metabolized to create energy.

If that ENERGY is balanced all will be well. If that ENERGY becomes unbalanced, things will not be okay.

That is all we are: ENERGY.

Secondly, let us look at EMOTION.

You will probably be surprised to hear that the day that I began to get well was the day that I began to figure out that, "for me", ENERGY and EMOTION were one and the same thing.

If you were to ask a group of people in a room what EMOTIONS are, the strong likelihood is that they will come up with words like anger, hurt, sad, happy, etc.

I am not saying that they would be wrong, but with my new understanding I was beginning to look at emotions with a much wider lens.

The word EMOTION has existed in the English language since the 17th century, originating as a translation of the French word emotion, meaning a physical disturbance. This was based on the Latin word emovere which meant moving out (e-motion = energy moving). So, for me (and I found this a really helpful way of understanding) EMOTIONS mean a physical movement and displacement of ENERGY in the body.

EMOTIONS go right back through the animal kingdom almost to

the beginning of time. For that reason, we need to understand them more than we do. Rational brain and the arrival of language happened a long time after emotionality and biology.

With this new language we attempted to put words to what we were feeling, without really understanding the feelings, and in many cases, leading to a distortion of the story.

So, what are EMOTIONS?

EMOTIONS are something that you feel in the body and in the brain.

Remember when the twig snapped and the message was sent down the brain stem to the Sympathetic Nervous System? All the cells were activated, and most of the body's energy was displaced from the visceral block to the reflex block.

All the blood and oxygen (energy) were displaced and moved to different locations purely for survival.

The sensations (feelings) that go with this can be so intense, but they have to be; they are designed to get you to take instant action to get away from the perceived danger.

So, what you are feeling is energy moving, e-movere, EMOTIONS.

There is no language for them. For real wellness this needs to be understood; you cannot rationalize your way out of an EMOTION.

The third word that is intrinsically connected to ENERGY and EMOTION is MOOD.

One of the most helpful ways I discovered that helped me to understand my story was to see MOOD as a state of ENERGY.

LOW MOOD EQUALS LOW ENERGY

HIGH MOOD EQUALS HIGH ENERGY

FOR BALANCED MOOD WE NEED BALANCED ENERGY.

So, the instinct of FEAR "everything is not going to be okay", created an EMOTION (energy moving) to help us react and deal with the perception of an incoming threat of danger. Instantly we created a SURVIVAL RESPONSE.

Darwin maintained that humans subconsciously created one of three avoidance behaviors to escape from danger. His thinking was that once the perceived moment of danger arrived, they resorted to one of three automatic responses:

The first was FIGHT, and one stood and fought the danger (in our ancestor's case, the tiger). In order for this to happen, one needed to be pumped up and energies (blood, oxygen, hormones, chemicals) had to be redirected to different areas of the body and brain to maximize the chances of winning the fight and surviving.

HIGH ENERGY = HIGH MOOD

The second was FLIGHT, and one ran from the perceived danger. Also, in order for this to happen, one needed to be pumped up and energies (blood, hormones, chemicals, oxygen) had to be redirected to different areas of the body and the brain to maximize the chances of surviving by avoiding and getting away from the danger.

HIGH ENERGY = HIGH MOOD

The third was FREEZE; you froze on the spot, held your breath and tried to blend into the environment, hoping that you would not be seen.

LOW ENERGY = LOW MOOD.

These three avoidance behaviors have adapted and evolved to shape almost every aspect of human behavior, some for good and some not so good.

You can see, hopefully, that we have an amazing, evolutionary, in-built mechanism for survival in moments of danger.

Firstly, the instinct of FEAR lets us know that everything is not okay, and is not going to be okay if we do not take immediate action.

Secondly, with EMOTION extra energy is created and diverted to different areas of the body and brain to help us escape and survive.

Thirdly, we subconsciously created a BEHAVIOUR to help us to avoid and survive.

It is the lack of awareness of these learned behaviors and attachments that can potentially mess up our lives. The fear response is only a short-term mechanism for survival, and if it is in balance we will survive and evolve. However, if the fear response is being activated on a continual basis it will have massive consequences for our ability to survive and evolve, as we are not programmed to be in a fear response over an extended period of time.

ANXIETY: THE GREATEST PROBLEM OF THE TWENTY-FIRST CENTURY

ANXIETY is probably one of the most talked-about words in recent modern times. And yet I would think it is fair to say it is also one of the most misunderstood words in modern times. In my quest for recovery from the trauma of dealing with my own story of life, I discovered that the best way of understanding anxiety was to have a really good understanding of all the things I have spoken about in the previous pages.

So, I talked about the instinctive FEAR response that the body and the brain have to a perception of danger. I outlined the survival state that the body goes into as energy is relocated and redistributed, and also the unpleasant feeling that goes with this process (which is necessary to get you to react).

This sensation of UNEASE that we experience as all of this is happening, that sensation of UNEASE is ANXIETY.

We need a little bit of this UNEASE (ANXIETY) as it is important to us. It keeps us focused in the moment; it gets the job done, it helps us to pay attention to getting the important things started and completed.

Managed anxiety keeps the balance between Blue Zone and Red Zone at an optimum, and keeps us aware.

We need both the Blue Zone and the Red Zone working together in balance. This is why humans have two minds, one mind for feeling and the other one for thinking. This is why evolution has developed and supported the need for two minds. Feelings (Red Zone) take care of our desires and needs in the present moment, while rational thinking (Blue Zone) is looking after our welfare and interests in the future.

If rationality (Blue Zone) did not exist, we would definitely be in a bad way. We would lose interest in anything that does not provide us with instant pleasure. We would not be creative or productive. We would have no choices. We would simply slip into a life of addiction, attachments and maladaptive behaviors that would kill us even before we managed to procreate.

But without emotionality (Red Zone) we would not survive either. Emotional brain is providing us with immediate signals that help us to be alert to danger and survive. If our emotional brain was not working, we would be badly burned every time we put our hand in a fire, as our emotional brain would not remember to pull it out.

Back in our hunter-gatherer times the instinct of FEAR was our friend and greatest ally. We very seldom had to use it, and even if we did it was a short-term response just to help us deal with the immediate danger, and then everything all came back to balance.

Now in the modern postindustrial technologically-driven world, it has become our greatest enemy and has the potential to destroy our species, as we are not psychologically, emotionally, or biologically programmed to live in a world of fear all day every day.

Because we live in such an angry, confrontational, incredibly anxious, worried, troubled and fearful world nearly all the time now, the human organism is stuck in survival mode.

If an organism is stuck in the Red Zone, its energies are focused on fighting unseen enemies.

If we are spending too much time in the Red Zone (which a lot of people are now), incrementally over time we lose touch with the Blue Zone and we begin to lose the Blue Zone function. Our thinking becomes irrational (use it or lose it). An extended time in the emotional brain and we eventually become paranoid.

It becomes all about "me" because it is now all about "your" survival. Our thinking becomes linear and narrow, as we are constantly trying to seek out where the threat is coming from.

We start to look outside of ourselves for solutions, as we cannot cope with what we are feeling due to the constant relocation of energies.

This leaves no room for nurture, care and love. For us humans, it means that for as long as the mind is defending itself against invisible threats, our closest relationships are threatened, along with our ability to envision, create ideas, set goals, play, learn and pay attention to each other's needs. We are losing the Blue Zone function.

While all of this is happening in the mind and the brain, the hypothalamus keeps sending messages down the brain stem to let the cells know that danger is imminent (even though in the majority of cases there is no danger; they are just false perceptions, but our brain does not know the difference).

The protein pathways in the cells are being constantly activated (unnecessarily).

Eventually, the protein signals become distorted and out of sync with the environment, and all of this constant UNEASE (ANXIETY) becomes the DISEASE of mind and body.

We experience our most devastating emotions as gut-wrenching feelings and heartbreak. We have a feeling as if our chest is collapsing inwards or that we have been kicked in the stomach, and these feelings over time become unbearable.

We will do anything to make these awful feelings in our visceral block go away, whether it is clinging and cloying to another human being, resorting to comfort eating to escape this feeling of not belonging to myself, getting out of our mind on drugs or alcohol, or taking a knife to the skin to replace the overwhelming sensations of energies moving in the body, with definable sensations.

When the alarm bell of the Red Zone keeps signaling that we are in danger, and our Red Zone and Blue Zone are in conflict (as they are constantly as we now live in a world of fear) a tug-of-war ensues. The paradox here is that the more we spend our lives in anxiety, fear and conflict, the more we live in the Red Zone. The more we live in the

Red Zone the more we keep reconnecting to our stored and unacknowledged bad memories in the hippocampus, which keeps sending signals to the cells that danger is imminent and now we feel even worse.

And so, the cycle continues. This is largely played out in the theatre of visceral experience—our gut, our heart, our lungs—and will lead to physical irritation and pain as well as psychological/emotional misery.

When we live in a constant state of fear and heightened anxiety, we lose our conscious awareness. Consciousness is a balance of internal awareness and external awareness; in other words, "Love yourself, but love your neighbor as well".

Unfortunately, this is a concept that has been severely eroded, as more and more our culture teaches us to focus on personal uniqueness.

This has been to our detriment, because at a deeper level we barely exist as individual organisms. Our brains are designed and evolved to help us function as members of a clan. In our history, the importance could not be understated of coming together within the clan and being able to communicate and work together to advance our evolution as human beings. We have always had someplace to belong, and the clan has always been the centerpiece for belonging. The human condition will do anything to belong.

In heightened states of anxiety and fear, it is very difficult to feel this sense of belonging. We feel disconnected from ourselves and others. Our internal environments are in crisis, which is mirrored by the crisis that faces our external environments.

While our system is in a heightened state of unease (anxiety) over a long period of time (which it is not designed to be) our five senses overstimulate. As a result, we have become much more sensitive to environmental signals, which is creating a heightened sensitivity in humans and society that is reactive most of the time now.

We can see that because of our programming and our evolution over many millions of years, we are triggered to respond to the threat of danger immediately, at a given instant. However, the stress went away quickly as you either fought the tiger or you ran away from the tiger, and you learned to associate sounds, sights and places with the danger and avoid them in the future.

Unfortunately, as I discussed earlier, our brain is unable to distinguish the difference between reality and the perception of reality. Therefore, if the messaging that we are receiving twenty-four hours a day, seven days a week is fear and fear-based, we are obviously going to respond in an anxious way, because anxiety is just a natural response or behavior that has become maladaptive. Fear has taken over society.

This is the accepted point of view from a neuroscientific understanding with some additional colorations of my own. This view allowed me to understand how anxiety was ever-present in both me and in my family story. In essence I had lived my entire life in the Red Zone, so in effect, I would say, I became the way I was programmed.

As I said, these are the basic established facts of the evolution of our modern brain in as much as it can be understood. There are vast areas of our brain that we do not know anything about.

However, this is the mundane physical understanding, and no matter how many workshops, study courses, and worldwide journeys of seeking knowledge and information I was to make, cognitive learning on its own was not enough for me to achieve wellness. However, it was necessary as it allowed me to begin to understand myself as a total human in all its complexity and splendid glory.

The revelation that changed everything for me came when I encountered:

Paddy Rafter's *48 Acts Toward a New Way of Living*.

This was because I was elevated from the purely physical to a deeply personal, spiritual and instinctual awareness

I was enabled to enact a program for living.

I was enabled to achieve a higher level of consciousness.

I was enabled to gain possession of tools and different ways of thinking and experiencing to allow me to have a deeper understanding of myself.

I saw the benefit that this would bring to people right across the spectrum, from the deeply troubled to the self-diagnosed healthy, and I saw the immense value of the 48 Acts.

Therefore, I feel compelled to disseminate Paddy's message—in other words, the message contained in the 48 Acts— as they pertained to me so that all others might benefit.

THE LAYMAN'S GUIDE TO
THE SIXTEEN AXIOMS

I
"LIFE IS FULL OF SUFFERING."

What is suffering? Suffering can be described as a "conscious endurance of pain or distress." To understand suffering in this way helps us to understand that suffering is reality and that there is no escaping this reality. What is equally true is that our life is full of suffering.

So, understanding suffering as is pointed out in this Act is our road to reality, and what this Act helped me to understand is that I was looking at suffering the wrong way around. I saw suffering as something to be feared, to be avoided, to be denied. But in actual fact, through this Act I came to understand that suffering is our great teacher and that the more we can face and try to understand our suffering and indeed the suffering of the world, the more that suffering will dissipate.

Whether we like it or not, our life is full of suffering. The moment I was born I endured my first pain and distress (suffering) due to the fact that I experienced my first loss in life. The loss of the safety and comfort, peace and sanctuary of my mother's womb. And if you really think about it, from that moment on, our life is all about loss.

The loss of childhood.

Loss through leaving home for the first time.

Loss of friendships.
Loss of relationships.
Loss through sickness and illness.
Loss of hope.
Loss of voice.
Loss through bereavement.
Loss of trust in self and in others.
Loss of dignity.
Loss of employment.
Loss of self through abuse and violence.

On every step of the journey, we encounter loss, and each one of these losses brings with it great pain and distress. This pain and distress, if it is not understood and acknowledged, will ultimately become our suffering, which can and often does last a lifetime until finally we have our ultimate loss, death. In many ways our wellness throughout our life will be determined by our ability to adapt, when change and loss come into our lives. If we do not learn to behave and adapt from an early age to our life losses, over time our behaviors can and often do become maladaptive. It is these maladaptive behaviors which can cause difficulties in our lives on an ongoing basis.

When we do not have the awareness or the language to understand and to articulate the different sensations and feelings that go with these losses, the painful memories are stored in our Red Zone. The next time I experience a loss of any kind, I immediately open up the storage department of the hippocampus, and all my other unacknowledged losses come flooding into the present moment. This can and often does make everything feel an awful lot worse than it actually is at that moment and time.

This all happens automatically, and the body is now gone into the fear response. Energies are relocated all over the body, and this process brings about a great discomfort in mind and body.

This feeling of great discomfort serves a purpose, as it is designed to get us to react to a perception that everything is not going to be okay, and is preparing the body for the fight, flight or freeze response for survival.

Because nobody ever taught us this, and in order to escape from these ongoing unpleasant feelings of discomfort, over time we form attachments to people, possessions, drugs, alcohol, sex, gambling, anger, anything really (in my case, education and a quest for knowledge in order to get approval and appreciation from people) to help us escape from the reality of what we are feeling and cannot understand.

These are what addictions are, an escape from reality, and the forming of attachments to try to get some alleviation from the constant pain and distress (suffering) that we are experiencing.

I would never have realized that I was addicted. I always saw addiction as drugs or alcohol or sex or gambling, but I was wrong. I learned from this Act that I was addicted to the most powerful drug of all in the world today, the drug of approval and appreciation. This has the exact same effect on the workings of the brain as alcohol or drugs, because it is based on fear. The fear of not being good enough, the fear of not being liked, the fear that people might know, the fear that people might think we were poor (I could go on and on). But ultimately these attachments were just an escape from my constant feelings of pain and distress.

I subsequently learned through these Acts that it was the attachments that were making me sick, not the feelings or what happened in childhood, and that in order to be well I had to learn to become aware of these attachments and gradually learn to let them go one by one.

Once I began to understand suffering in this way, and started to make the necessary adjustments in my life, the pain and distress began to ease.

They never fully go away, and this is important to understand. What changes is that when the inevitable losses come in your life, which they will, you will not avoid them anymore. Anyway, I would not want to avoid them anymore, as it was the avoidance that made me sick.

I learned that if I just sat with what was disturbing me at a particular moment and time, no matter how awful the sensations felt, they could not do me any harm. All they are is feelings, and feelings cannot do me any harm. It was the attachments and the behaviors that I learned to escape these awful sensations that were making me sick.

Over time, I eventually began to see fear and suffering as my friends. I learned to embrace them, understand them, to not be afraid of them and learn to live with them and deal with them in the present.

This over time alleviated the feelings of pain and distress, made me less fearful of the future, and gave me an ability to deal with feelings of the past when they arrived uninvited.

Through this Act I learned that suffering is not something handed to us by "God"; suffering is caused by people through action or inaction. The good news is that through becoming aware, there is something that everyone can do to help alleviate this pandemic of unhappiness that permeates throughout the world.

2
"YOUR LIFE IS NOT ABOUT YOU."

The one thing I would never have said is that my life was about me.

My life could not have been about me; sure, I was the ultimate placater, the ultimate fixer, everybody's friend. I had spent my life trying to make a difference in the lives of other people, and ultimately heal the world. All my good dreams as a child were all about growing up to be some sort of superhero and going on to making a big difference in a positive way in the lives of people. I got into massive debt, I remortgaged the house, I almost died trying to achieve this. Of course, this was not about me; how could anyone even think that? This was about saving everybody else.

Boy did I get that wrong.

This, as you can imagine, was a really difficult Act for me to get my head around. I was the good child, I was the one who was hurt as a child, how could this be my fault. None of these things should have happened. I was the victim.

Wrong.

I was not the victim. I was victimized. There is a great difference. When I began to understand the difference, I began to get well. Everybody in life at some point or other has been victimized, but not everyone spends the rest of their life being a victim. I did not realize it for a long time, but I can see now that being a victim actually suited me. It invoked sympathy for me from people when I would tell my life story. People told me I was "great", "very brave", "a beacon of shining light in the world". They reinforced my narrative and my dreams that I was growing up to be a superhero who was making a difference in the world. I would feel approved and appreciated.

It facilitated me to live in denial and never have to look at my own deep darkness; sure why would I do that? I was a victim; I could always blame somebody else for how I was feeling and for where I was in my life.

Through this particular Act I became aware that blame was really an attachment, because as long as I had somebody to blame, well, then I never had to look at myself and my own behaviors. All of this was really only pushing my hurt, anger, loneliness, shame and guilt deeper into my subconscious. It is so easy to be a victim; it is a great place to hide and not have to take any personal responsibility.

Everybody wants to hear our story and we become some sort of a hero, but really people were often only hijacking our narrative for their own selfish purposes. This was most definitely my experience, and this was a very difficult thing to realize as in a way it was almost like being abused all over again.

But the truth is, that no matter what happened all of those years ago, these stored memories and feelings are mine. I am the only one who can do something about them. I had to learn not to measure myself by what other people thought and felt about me.

My whole life was about pleasing other people and wanting everybody to love me, because the truth was, I did not love myself. But this was the only way I could be happy. I confused approval and appreciation with happiness. I wanted happiness more than anything in the world.

However, I learned through this Act that the opposite was the case. I was an addictive person. I was addicted to emotive behavior, which was only destined to make me more unhappy because it was all about me.

I can see that all so clearly now. I could be giving a presentation to four or five hundred people, and at the end there would be a great big standing ovation, but all I ever saw was the person who did not stand up, or who did not appear to enjoy it. I would be devastated, and it would drive me even deeper into a world of not being liked or loved. This meant I now had to work harder to please people. Pretty soon my life became unmanageable and devoid of any contentment and happiness. But I believed that if I tried even harder, I would eventually find happiness. The reality is that I was depending on people and external sources to make me happy.

The real truth is that it was all about my false ego, my false beliefs, my false assumptions, based on a false input from a false source, and that was not reality. I had to learn to get into reality, and that is very difficult to do.

Why?

Because reality can be a very painful place to be, which is why we spend our lives escaping from reality into an addictive life of destructive behaviors which can cause great harm to ourselves and to others.

Although reality in the short term can be a painful place, learning to live in reality in the long term can be life-changing (for the good).

The first mantra I learned to say repeatedly to myself over and over again was:

"I AM NOT A VICTIM".

I was hurt as a child and bad things happened, but guess what? The same can be said for millions of people in the world today. Ultimately life is unfair, that's a fact whether we like it or not. It is not my job to run all over the world to balance the scales of justice, just so I can feel better.

Nobody is to blame; yes, somebody did me wrong, but I can't change that now. It is as it is.

I have spent a significant amount of time trying to fully understand and comprehend the message of this Act. To really get a deeper meaning I had to learn to understand it, not only cognitively, but also in an instinctual, gut-knowing way as well. Even with all I knew, I still struggled with the concept.

I asked myself the question, "How is it any good to me if my life is not about me?" I am sure anybody reading this would ask the same question. I mean, what is the point? Because even in doing this, it is still all about "me" and "me" trying to get well, which then leads to the question,

"If it is not about me, who is it about?"

But this is where constant reflection and challenging myself to see and understand things differently was to be of great benefit.

Over a period of time, I began to realize that really what it was about was the inner me, not the outer me. It was about the inner me within the connection of all things, all people.

What it is not about is the attachments, the outer me.

A lot of times when we are cognitively trying to figure out and understand things in our head, we invariably end up with more questions than answers.

I got to a point where I ceased to try to find the answer to this Act cognitively. As the program was suggesting, I was beginning to learn to listen to my gut and my instincts a little bit more, and trust that in time the answer would reveal itself to me.

I am sure I must have had all of these 48 Acts written and rewritten dozens of times when the answer came to me.

I was at a family wedding, and while I was out on the floor dancing with my daughter, she remarked to me that she had "never seen me so relaxed on the dance floor and so in sync with people and the music".

This was to prove to be my eureka moment. For most of my life when I would on occasion be at a dance, I turned up in one of two ways:

In my earlier years, I would be the person shyly and quietly dancing on the corner of the dance floor, trying to be anonymous, not wanting to bring attention to myself. But in essence it was really about what other people thought of me, so yes, it was all about me. The upshot was I never really enjoyed myself. I held myself back, as what other people thought of me was more important.

As I got older and my addiction to approval, appreciation and attention was increasing exponentially, I became the exact opposite on the dance floor. I was the one in the brighter than bright colors, dancing outrageously in the center of the dance floor, just to be seen.

It was all about me. I was not enjoying it as I always felt it had to be a performance.

Now, as pointed out by my daughter, I was on the dance floor in a communal sense. It was not about me anymore. I was actually enjoying myself, purely because it was not about me. I was enjoying the music and the company and the existence of the greater energy, purely from my body and gut, no longer in my head, no longer perceiving what other people thought. I was able to be in the moment, and the irony of it was that I had arrived organically in the moment without even cognitively thinking about it.

❦ 3 ❦
"THERE IS A POWER GREATER THAN YOURSELF."

Nearly everybody who hears this, automatically thinks of God in some form or another. This immediately causes problems because in the modern postindustrial world, God has a bad name and most people think that there is a talk on Religion imminent.

This is most definitely what I would have believed.

Why?

I grew up in a patriarchal family where the rules and the beliefs were authenticated by the religious patriarchy. These beliefs were that God the Father was the Almighty and must be obeyed at all times. My mother and father were held accountable to God, and blind obedience was a virtue. My parents were to be honored as if they were God's ("Thou shalt honor thy father and mother"). We as children were never allowed to raise our voices, or express anger or opinions towards our parents. And within that parental dyad itself there was a hierarchy.

Women were subject to and had to obey their husbands. Both my parents had a God-given right to inflict corporal punishment on their children. The golden rules in our family growing up were, "Do not talk", "Do not trust", and "Do not feel". Our moral and ethical values were enshrined within the man made diktat of the Ten Commandments. Everything was black or white, right or wrong, and every sin was punished. This was the way I was programmed to experience the world as a child.

I believed that God was all powerful and loving, and then all of a sudden, my beliefs and trust in that process were severely challenged when I was sexually abused by a religious person who worked for and who had a direct line to this God.

It was only decades later, when I was in a desperate dark hole, that I came across Paddy Rafter and the 48 Acts and began to understand God and higher power in a different and more examined way.

The first thing that I learned was that confusing religion, clerics and humans with God was a huge mistake, because they are not the same thing. God has nothing to do with any of these things irrespective of whether God exists or not. These atrocities that happen in the world are the actions of men, men's greed, men's desire, and men's needs. They have nothing to do with God. But because we have free will, it is as it is. Were there a God and he chose to intervene, we would cease to be human. We could not be human and be automated; they are obviously two separate things.

Through this Act, I began to look at this greater power in a different way, and in looking at it with a more lateral viewpoint I was able to embrace it into my own wellbeing program.

Embracing the Scientific View.

It is indisputable from a scientific point of view that there is a power greater than me in the world. From a physics point of view, the earth, the sun, etc., are all part of the solar system. The solar system is perhaps one of two billion solar systems in our galaxy. Our galaxy is a medium-sized galaxy that is perhaps one of three or four billion galaxies in the observable universe.

As you can see, we are only a tiny speck in the midst of this vastness, so it goes without saying there has to be a power greater than ourselves, but we do not have to be able to name it, and this is the key.

The key is just to know and give thanks to something that is obviously holding everything together.

This was the point where I began to equate the words power and energy. I began to realize that what worked for me was coming to the conclusion that there was an energy greater than me in the world. There has to be. There has to be an infinite energy source that I could plug into to renew my energy.

I began to see myself as a small unit of energy, a small connection of atoms, and I interact with the world around me as all energy does. All energy is either negative or positive. I just had to learn how to plug into this source of energy.

But how do I tap into this powerful source of energy? One of the stumbling blocks for me was that through my faulty belief system and faulty programming I believed that this power source was God of creation.

I had to adhere to all of these diktats that were handed down by middle men (priests and clerics) in order to receive this energy or the so called "grace of God". That is what I was taught.

When I was working through these Acts, which helped me to examine my own faulty beliefs and faulty thinking's that were making me sick, I was fascinated with the story of the uncovering of massive underground structures that were excavated in Gobekli Tepe in Turkey in 1963.

"Twelve thousand years ago, Gobekli Tepe was built. Gobekli Tepe is in Turkey in the Middle East, where two continents meet. It is a large stone structure consisting of hundreds of massive pillars. Each pillar is approximately fifty tons in weight and richly decorated with both realistic and abstract anthropomorphic detail as well as reliefs of wild animals and flowers. Each pillar is T-shaped, and they are set in a large circle over a twenty-acre site.

Extraordinarily, this incredible structure was built by nomadic peoples. Because of its enormous size, it required a great number of clans to work together to create it. Thus, they set aside their ancient enmities and worked harmoniously, though they were mortal enemies.

How could this be possible? Not just the enormous amount of physical labor involved, and the huge numbers of people required over a sustained period of time. More importantly for us: how could they set aside their mutual hate to undertake this task?

In their gratitude, and because of their way of life in nature and their experiential knowledge, they created a communal space where they could interact with the power that was all around them and in them, in what they could see, and in what they could not see but intuit and experience on a daily basis. The power of the essence. The power of being and existence that they lived with every moment. They had no need for belief. They knew. They only had a need for acknowledgement of that which was real.

Therefore, they set aside millions of accumulated years of hate, in gratitude for the power of love, the love that sustained them every day. The enormous endeavor that they accomplished has come down to us, even today. This was the "Holy Mountain". Subsequently, we have had pyramids and sacred high places, holy mountains, temples and cathedrals. Gobekli Tepe and the surrounding sites were our first mass communal celebration places."

If they could complete these herculean tasks physically and spiritually twelve thousand years ago, then surely, we can do it in the twenty-first century. Surely, we can find the meaning of the power of being and love, and a God of existence within this. Surely, we can set aside our hatred and our clan and country identities and work together with this power, this energy and save ourselves and our planet from spiritual and physical destruction

This was God and without this God or power or energy (whatever you want to call it) being in balance, we or the planet would not have survived. It was only thousands of years later, when the ideologies of religions were created, that we began to see a God of creation rather than what it was for millennia: a God of existence.

I for one would not condemn a person's religion or ideology purely because of my experience. Indeed, many of these religions and ideologies had many well-intentioned people involved who did bring goodness. However, it is incontrovertibly true that if you stand back and look at every major conflict and war right up to the present day, you will see ideologies and religion at the center of every one of them, and in most cases did nothing but create divisiveness.

I spent most of my life feeling so confused, wondering why God had let me down and why God let such awful things happen in the world until I discovered through this Act that I was looking at God in the wrong way. It was not God that was doing all of this, it was humans, hiding behind the name of their so called "God".

You can go back through every war and conflict in the world, in particular in the last ten to twelve thousand years since we first started to live in towns and cities, and without exception every conflict has religion and ideologies at its core.

But the sad thing is that the world is so polarized at this moment, and is so full of ideologies (such as religions, capitalism, consumerism, me culture, communism, race wars, gender wars, cancel culture, etc.) and divisiveness and we are getting sicker by the day.

But there is something that we can do, we must try to find a way of coming together as one.

Our hunter-gatherer ancestors figured this out over twelve thousand years ago. They were able to come together as one (from and with literally nothing) to create these massive structures, where people gave thanksgiving and praise to this greater power that they knew instinctively was vital for the survival and evolution of humankind.

Over time and by a different understanding, I came to the realization that there was a power greater than me, that was not just, given titles or glorification, but that I could just accept, there just is. All I had to do was to accept the obvious.

4
"YOU HAVE EVERYTHING YOU NEED AT YOUR DISPOSAL TO BE HAPPY. YOU JUST DON'T KNOW IT."

When I first read this particular Act, I discovered that I had never understood what happiness really was. I had a very distorted view of happiness based on my faulty childhood programming that led me to believe that I could never be happy unless I made everybody else happy.

My life was about meeting other people's needs, in order for my own needs to be satisfied. In other words, If I can make everybody else happy, well then, I can be happy too. I never realized I was addicted to the drug of approval and appreciation. I just wanted to be liked and loved.

In hindsight, this view of the world has not worked out very well for me. I had become so intoxicated by my desire to be highly educated and know everything that was to be known about the human condition, that I did not realize that my continuous onward rush to get this knowledge and spread the word, almost like a messiah, was what was actually making me very sick. I had an insatiable appetite for knowledge and information.

I believed the powerful message of the capitalist consumer model.

"If you obtain all of these things, you will be happy."

But the problem was the more I got, the unhappier I became. The more unhappy I became, the more money I spent.

It was like a drug. I was buying an illusion. It was never going to make me happy.

I sought more.

I spent more money (money I did not have).

I spent huge money on things, and some of the time I never even checked properly to see if they were real.

I became more unhappy.

On the very rare occasion that I had some awareness of not being well, I bought into the wellness industry that was giving me the same message.

I spent a fortune on wellness programs, but they made me even more unhappy. When I stopped to "live in the present moment", "the place where happiness exists" (the mantra sold to me by people who I now know were selling snake oil), I nearly went mad altogether.

When I would stop in the moment to "look inside of myself", all I saw was an incredible black hole of darkness from which I had spent my whole life running away. None of this "living in the moment" nonsense for me. The moment for me was so painful, why would I want to live there? Or, for that reason, why would anyone want to live there?

So, what did I do? Continued on my journey of seeking happiness outside of myself—and believe you me, there were plenty of people who had happiness for sale! I craved this way of life that people were willing to sell to me.

It is often only when a terrible crisis is forced upon us, one that literally stops us in our tracks, that we end up in a position in which, if we do not stop, we will die.

When this happened to me, I was very fortuitous to have come across Paddy Rafter and his teachings.

He challenged and allowed me to:

Stop and examine what I really wanted, why I wanted it, and what is it really doing for me?

Become aware off and understand the awful fear and anxiety I constantly lived in.

As a result, I learned to see the world as it really was, rather than the way I wanted it to be.

I learned to stay at home and tend the garden, rather than continually running away and getting lost in the jungle.

I had to learn to deprogram.

I became happy by undoing, not doing.

I learned to stay in and trust the moment, and over time as I learned to do that, I found my way into the happiness within.

I discovered that we are born happy; it is a generic state. However, it is the things that happen to us on our journey, that we cannot understand or cope with, which causes us to build layers of shame, hurt, anger, guilt and isolation on top of this generic happiness. The more layers we build, the further we move away from this happiness and the more unhappy we become.

It is only over time as we gently remove and become aware of these layers, and learn not be afraid of the feelings they invoke within us, that we organically arrive into happiness, peace and contentment.

It takes time. It will not be perfect; do not expect it to be, because perfect does not exist. It is within learning to live with and accept our imperfections that we organically arrive into the happiness within us.

So, the truth is:

"You do have everything at your disposal to make you happy; you just never knew."

5

"YOUR SUFFERING IS CAUSED BY YOUR PROGRAMMING. THE KEY TO UNLOCKING YOUR PROGRAMMING IS KNOWLEDGE, UNDERSTANDING AND AWARENESS."

Your world view has been programmed.

The way you treat the world has been programmed.

Your reaction to the world has been programmed.

Your suffering is caused by your programming.

What is this programming I speak about?

Programming, in essence, is the way that we learned to experience the world as a child. It has to do with the information we received both covertly and overtly from our parents, guardians, and society in general.

This information is often the only way that we can experience the world, and we believe it to be true. Programming is also how we perceive this information.

Most of our conditioning and programming takes place in our families of origin and particularly in the information that we received before seven years of age, which was locked into our Red Zone. This programming runs our lives for better or for worse 95 per cent of the time.

A factor in this is how our families adapted to the impact of the ever changing and evolving environment both inside and outside of the family.

The 48 Acts, and in particular this Act, were challenging me to become more aware and have a greater understanding of my programming. It made great sense to me to look at my family of origin and see how growing up in a very anxious family had such an impact on my experience of the world thereafter.

As you will have read in the previous pages, every family has its own unique identity and its own story to tell, and indeed these stories can go back through many generations. There is no such thing as the perfect family even though I have met many who believed that their family was one. My family was a story of mental illness, addiction, anxiety, and sexual abuse.

I discovered through reading and understanding the work of many, that what happened was that within our family stories we subconsciously became characters. Because our mainstream education models do not teach us conscious awareness, we can often get locked into these characters and roles in a very unhealthy way for the rest of our lives.

These roles are not something that most people think about (a lot of people think they were born a certain way, but we most definitely are not). But if you stand back and look, there are four distinct roles that appear at some level or other in almost every family. Much has been written about these roles, and indeed I have read many of these great writers and their ideas. These are the roles that I could relate to best in my family of origin.

Firstly, many families have a joker, a funny little guy or gal, who quite often can grow up to be the life and soul of the party.

There is the good little child—often but not always the oldest—the responsible one, the serious one who can be identified as mammy's little hero.

There is the rebel, the one who will not conform.

And then there is the lost child, the one who learned not to make connections early on in life. It may be a child who, for whatever reason, experienced attachment issues with the mother or the father.

One problem with these roles is that the more difficulties the family may be experiencing either externally or internally, the more locked into the role each person can become, and subsequently the more maladaptive their behaviors become.

Take the joker for example. The joker's role, particularly in a family that may be struggling, is to use humor to escape from the reality of what is really going on. On the surface that can work really well for the child in that family, because it provides an avoidance and escape route from feeling any pain. Jokers tend to be cute, and they can use their charm or good humor to survive. As an adult, however, a person locked in the role can be hyperactive in relationships and will do anything to attract attention as a diversion from more serious things. They can also be fragile, as it turns out that this comedic role is a defensive wall and a way of avoiding feelings of insecurity, fear, and loneliness. A joker avoids making decisions, which can cause difficulties in maintaining relationships. Jokers crave approval and appreciation.

Ultimately this role can be programmed into the Red Zone and onto the hard drive of the subconscious as a way of survival. If not understood it can become a maladaptive behavior that we attach ourselves to (unknowingly) in order to help us escape the constant unease (anxiety) that we are experiencing within the family system. Within the context of Darwin's escape and avoidance model, this would be flight. It is a way of seeking approval and appreciation.

The lost child, meantime, will struggle to find any sense of belonging. This is the child who struggles to make connections within the family, and who can become hyper-independent, even withdrawn and aloof.

It may be the child who does not want to go out to play, or even the quiet one who is known as the "loner" in the school environment.

Because of this isolation they often do not develop social skills, which often makes it even harder to find belonging through friendships or relationships.

They are the ones who appear not to need other people—except that we all need other people. The lost child can often be seen as the good child as the lost child rarely causes any difficulties, and can be very compliant.

They tend not to give any hassle, and are often given approval and reward for that role; a parent can often say to other siblings, "Why can't you be like your brother/sister, he/she never gives us any hassle".

But the reward is to become programmed and even more enveloped into that frame of mind, often for the rest of their lives. And because they do not develop social skills along with their peers, they will continue to have difficulties forming relationships in adulthood, including if they go on to have children of their own.

Much the same as the joker, the role of the lost child can also be programmed onto the hard drive of the Red Zone as a way of survival. If not understood it can become a maladaptive behavior that we subconsciously form an attachment with, in order to escape the almost constant unease (anxiety) that we are experiencing within the family system. Within the context of Darwin's escape and avoidance model this would be "freeze". It is a way of seeking approval and appreciation.

The role of the rebel, on the other hand, is the most problematic for parents in a family where there is pain and difficulties, and is used to provide a distraction from what is really going on—except that where a joker provides comedy, a rebel adds tragedy.

So, imagine that a family is experiencing mum's depression or sickness, or dad's unemployment or alcoholism, or the anxiety that comes with the frantic pace of modern life. From early morning commutes to the cost of childcare, financial fragilities, pressures to have children involved in activities, all the things which families find difficult to talk about—the rebel will find ways of avoiding them, and in the process, he or she becomes the problem that is discussed at length.

This child may be acting out at school, the one who is constantly angry or fighting, or is antisocial at underage alcohol or drug parties. The rebel is often the one running away, refusing to be a part of the family, or being sullen, withdrawn, detached.

The rebel is often the most painful role to play out, as the behavior involved can often be so destructive. This role has the potential to bring a great deal of hurt and shame to the family, and deep-rooted feelings of guilt and shame to the rebel.

Not all rebels necessarily become antisocial or delinquent, but can often grow up feeling very hard done by: with a chip on their shoulder, cynical and angry, and feeling that the world owes them something all the time.

Anger can often become an attachment because the fear would be that if we let the anger go, we might be forced to look at our own hurts and insecurities.

Once again, the role of the rebel can often be programmed onto the hard drive of the Red Zone as a way of survival. If not understood it can become a maladaptive behavior that we attach ourselves to (subconsciously) in order to escape the constant unease (anxiety) that we experience within the family system. Within the context of Darwin's escape and avoidance model, this would be "fight". It is a way of seeking approval and appreciation.

Lastly (and this is the one I can relate to most, as it was me) there is the responsible one, or the good child. This is the child who is eager to please, and often takes over the mantle from a parent who might be unavailable through mental or physical illness, or maybe has departed the family home. He or she often becomes the third parent in the home, or the replacement parent if one of the parents has left, taking on the role to create meaning in his or her own life. And it does give meaning, as it invokes a lot of approval and positive reinforcement from people inside and outside of the home.

But the problem is that they can feel obliged to fill that role repeatedly, and can often feel an obligation to be good at everything.

Throughout all of this, however, for the good child there is a perpetual feeling of not being good enough, and when a good child leaves the family of origin, he or she can become a people pleaser. Feeling that a good child's role is to be responsible for everybody else's wellness and for keeping them happy, if everybody else is not happy, the good child is not happy. It is a way of seeking approval and appreciation.

These roles are evident in every culture, and you can also have combinations of them. It is important to say that there is nothing inherently wrong with these roles, and they are helpful ways of understanding why we are all so different.

Having said that, without awareness of the programming of these roles on the hard drive of the Red Zone, these roles can affect how we perceive and experience the world and are often the only lens in which we see and experience the world. This can cause us to live our lives in very unhealthy ways that can prevent us from becoming the kind of people we would like to be. Often, because of this programming in our family of origin, we can have a very narrow worldview and unrealistic expectations of how the world should act and react towards us.

What underpins these roles is a deep-rooted unease (anxiety), and it is this anxiety that can have a severe mental and physical impact on our lives afterwards.

In conclusion, let us reflect on how these programmed roles would be linked into the "survival behaviors" that Darwin spoke about.

FIGHT THE REBEL
HIGH ENERGY/MOOD
FLIGHT THE GOOD CHILD, THE JOKER
HIGH ENERGY/MOOD
FREEZE THE LOST CHILD
LOW ENERGY/MOOD

The great learning for me in this Act was that although I knew all of this knowledge cognitively, I did not have the proper understanding. You can't experience this cognitively; you can only fully experience it as an instinctive, gut-knowing, visceral happening.

Yes, I knew all the science about the energies being relocated in the body and the roles we adapt to escape and survive anxious feelings, which form our maladaptive behaviors over time. But what I never allowed myself to do, until I learned it in this program, was to allow myself to sit with and actually experience these feelings in my body, without rationalizing them in my head. Over time I learned to instinctively know from my gut that I was going to be okay. You can't think your way to recovery; you have to feel your way.

6
"TRAUMA IS PAIN CAUSED BY YOUR PERCEPTION OF CIRCUMSTANCES."

This particular Act really resonated with me. Having lived with and worked with trauma for over fifty years, it challenged me to look at trauma in a different way.

I have spent most of my life trying to get the answers for two questions:

Why did I have the feeling of this awful hole in the pit of my stomach all the time?

Why did I live my life with the constant feeling of a "nameless dread", and a constant sense of "impending doom"?

I will come to my new understanding of why this was in a moment, but what must be asked first is,

What is trauma?

The American Psychological Association defines it thus: "Trauma is an emotional response to a terrible event like an accident, violence, rape or natural disaster".

Of course, this is true, but I believe it is too narrow a definition. For me personally, what really helped me when I read this Act was to redefine my own understanding of trauma.

I worked on overseas missions with people who had all the symptoms of trauma, but during reflection they would say that they had never experienced a traumatic incident. There was no terrible event obvious to them in their working memory, but yet they would present in deep distress, pain and high anxiety.

The origin of the word trauma is the ancient Greek word trauma, and it has three meanings: wound, hurt, defeat.

The reality is that we have stored memories and feelings throughout our recorded history. Unacknowledged traumatic events that may have happened centuries ago can still cause people pain and distress in their lives today. We know this to be true, as a mother's fears and anxiety can be passed through the placenta to the unborn child in the perinatal experience.

I know this to be true from my own family of origin. My mother had the trauma of sexual abuse as a child, which needless to say in those days was never processed. So, the sexual abuse was the event. The trauma was the wound that was left behind, hidden in the stored memory department of the Red Zone. It is like geting a splinter in your finger, the splinter is the event, the splinter can be taken out, but the trauma is the wound that is left behind and can cause a lot of damage if not treated and cleansed.

Every time in the present moment that my mother would worry (perceive) that everything was not going to be okay, she would unknowingly be reconnecting to the stored original wound. It is not that she would remember the event, but she would reconnect to the feelings that went with the event, which in the present moment would confirm for her that everything is not going to be okay; and so the cycle continued. It was this constant state of unease, pain and distress that destroyed her life.

When my mother left her family of origin and formed her new family, unknown to her (and indeed anybody who does not have awareness) the anxiety came with her.

Ultimately, my mother's anxiety became our anxiety (unease). We became unwell as the constant high anxiety created an environment where we always felt that everything was not going to be okay, even though we did not know why.

So, the event was my mother's abuse. It was our perception that everything was not going to be okay, as each of us lived in the Red

Zone, that was causing the constant "fight, flight, or freeze" responses that were causing us pain and distress. Subsequently we subconsciously created maladaptive behaviors to help us to cope with this constant anxiety (unease). This family dynamic of high anxiety and pain stemmed from an event that happened many years before we were born.

For me in particular this Act provided great learning. As mentioned previously, I was sexually abused as a nine-year-old boy. The sexual abuse was the event. The trauma was the wound that was left in the storage part of my Red Zone. To escape the awful sensations of pain and distress that I lived with on a daily basis, I subconsciously created an avoidance behavior ("the good child") purely to survive. Every time later in life that I perceived that I was not matching up to my own expectations of myself, or that people did not like me, I would get even more anxious. Unknowingly I would be opening the storage department of my Red Zone and tapping into my original wound. This had the effect of making everything even more painful in the present moment, and would lock me even deeper into my maladaptive behaviors.

I learned through this Act that the only way I was going to become well was to make the journey back to the event of over fifty years ago and try to reconcile with my original wound, which I did.

Trauma, pain and hurt stem from our inability to live in the world today, irrespective of what caused our wounds. I genuinely believe that the world is traumatized now almost to the point of extinction.

All our lives now are outside the normal range of experiences. We live in constant fear, anxiety, conflict and anger in a world that has almost stopped caring, is going too fast, and is getting sicker by the day.

When you are anxious all the time, you live in a world of perceived threats which become your reality. This keeps the human organism locked in the Red Zone, which in turn keeps sending messages all over the brain and body that danger is imminent. Eventually, the constant relocation and redistribution of energies in the body allow the human organism to go out of balance and become sick.

At least in learning about myself in this way, I discovered that the constant hole in the pit of my stomach was energy being sucked away from my digestive system (the visceral block) and redirected to my reflex block for "fight, flight or freeze", which left that hollow feeling. At least I now knew that there was something I could do to alleviate this.

Also, the constant feeling of dread and impending doom was me being in the alert Red Zone mode all of the time, which meant that I was stuck in a threatened state and was always waiting for and expecting danger. Our perceptions have become our reality. This is very dangerous as we are not programmed psychologically, emotionally or biologically to live in fear all day every day.

Through knowledge, understanding and awareness, this can be changed to allow you to live a life of peace and contentment. You cannot change the event (what happened), but you can change your perception and understanding of your present circumstances.

Once again, in this Act I was learning to become more aware and more intuitive of the consequences of my perceptions. Before, when somebody would say something that I would not agree with, I would dismiss them because it did not fit with my perception. This Act has taught me to become more aware of my perceptions.

7

"BAD FEELINGS, BAD THINKING, TRAUMA AND PAIN CAUSE DAMAGING RESPONSES IN YOU, LEADING YOU TO EVER GREATER LIFE-CHANGING REACTION EVENTS, PAIN AND SUFFERING."

This Act for me was like a deeper development of Act Six. It gave me an extra insight into how trauma played out in my life; that insight was of great benefit, and added immeasurably to what I already knew.

I have spent a good chunk of my lifetime feeling bad, thinking irrationally, and reacting to these thoughts and feelings in a very damaging way. Funnily enough, when you exist in that world over a long period of time, particularly from childhood to adulthood, it just becomes normative and you genuinely believe that this is the way it is supposed to be.

As you can see from Act Six, when you have had traumatic events in your life, or you grow up in a very traumatic environment, your programming and your perceptions can become really faulty, and your life can become very illogical and damaging. The more irrational your life becomes, the more damaging your reactions can become, and the cycle continues. From the outsider's perspective this looks completely illogical as they can see the damage this is causing; but the truth is that from the addict's perspective this is very logical, as this is the way they have learned to escape from their internal reality. When I mention the word addict, I am talking about all of us as we are all somewhere on a continuum.

What do I mean by this?

Let us recap from earlier in this book.

We all have a mind and a body. Part of the problem is that we have two minds, and I call them the Blue Zone which is our rational brain, and the Red Zone which is our emotional/survival brain.

The mind determines what happens in our body.

For wellness of mind and body there must be balance between the Blue Zone and the Red Zone.

Picture, if you will, a straight line running from the very front of our Blue Zone the whole way to the very back end of our Red Zone. This straight line is what I call a continuum. For wellness of mind and body, we need to be somewhere in the middle of this continuum.

If we spend too much time in the Blue Zone, over time we learn to rationalize everything, and our thinking becomes very narrow and ultimately very polarized. We have a very linear view of people and the world. Our thinking believes everything is either black and white, or right or wrong, with absolutely no middle ground. It is our way or no way. We can become cold, detached and devoid of any feelings. We most definitely will not feel good about ourselves or the world.

By the same token, if we spend too much time in the Red Zone, we incrementally lose touch with the Blue Zone, and our thinking becomes irrational. The more anxious we become, the more irrational our thinking becomes. The more we retreat into the Red Zone, the more we reconnect to the stored memories that we are trying to avoid in the first place. The key receptors continue to send messages down through the brainstem to the ANS through the "fight, flight or freeze" reactions to form a whole-body cellular response.

The relocation of energies around the body to help us escape from the perceived threat has a most uncomfortable feeling, which makes us feel awful.

Because we do not understand and cannot cope with these bad feelings we connect to our learned maladaptive behaviors and attachments to escape how we are feeling.

As our thinking becomes more irrational, our behavior becomes more irrational, irresponsible, impulsive, compulsive, and sometimes reckless. From my own experience I do believe that there is a small part of us that knows we are doing wrong, but it is just that it is like being caught in a spider's web; sometimes the more we try to get out of it, the more we get sucked in.

In substance and behavioral addiction, people will tell us how "bad" our behaviors are, and how we are "damaging" other people's lives, which brings into play guilt and shame, two very corrosive emotions.

As this cycle continues, the subsequent judgements by other people (not that we need their judgement, as we become very good at judging ourselves anyway) make us feel even worse, so our responses become even more damaging and much more reactive, which inevitably leads to even greater life-changing reaction events and even more pain and suffering. Even if there is a part of us that wants to get out of this cycle, the subsequent fear of judgement, shame and guilt contrives to lock us in even more.

When we arrive in this space, we do not see the logic of what we are doing; scientifically, how could we? We have completely disconnected from the Blue Zone where our logic and rationale are housed.

We are all at some point on this continuum.

The more anxious the person becomes, the more they move into the Red Zone; but the good news is that we can learn to get back into the middle and find a balance between Red Zone and Blue Zone.

You can see the science behind all of this from what I have written in this Act; but why, for me, did it not work on its own? After all, I had over thirty years of professional and experiential learning in the battlefields of the world. So why did it work when I read it in this program?

Firstly, I would credit the starkness of reality in the way it was written.

Secondly, the progression of the sequencing from the previous Acts gave me a foundation that I could understand in a more intimate, experiential, gut-knowing way.

In other words, I understood it not just cognitively as I had always done, but in a much deeper way. This was because my own experiences were triggered, so I understood it in a different way than heretofore.

It is indisputable this worked. It enhanced what I already knew. I had to look at the meanings of bad feeling and bad thinking and what their consequences were for me.

I understood differently, through a gut knowing, that this was not something written on a page, but felt deep inside of me.

8
"ADDICTION AND MALADAPTIVE BEHAVIORS ARE A RESPONSE TO TRAUMA AND PAIN."

Nobody sets out to be an addict, an abuser, a fraud, a murderer, etc. Something happens on our journey to bring us there. Maladaptive behaviors and addictions are a response to pain and trauma, and can lead us to become very unwell with potentially calamitous consequences.

As has been said previously, the most important thing to take from this Act is that it is not our fault. Our responses to pain and trauma are due to our programming , and we are not responsible for our programming.

However, now that we have this information and can know and think about these things, our continued maladaptive behavior is our fault if we fail to act on our newly acquired knowledge.

This is a fact, this is true; once we become aware, we are 100 per cent responsible for any future consequences for our actions and behaviors. I know from my own experience that this is very difficult, as it is often the first time that we have had to look at ourselves in this way.

We do not have to fully accept everything at this point (I couldn't), but we just need to accept that it is a possibility, and tell ourselves, "Although I may have felt powerless up to now, and yes, my life is a mess, I do not want to live like this anymore. I just need to make a start".

One of the difficulties I experienced whilst starting on this journey of the 48 Acts was having to live in reality, instead of perceptions. When I was perceiving everything, I constantly lived in my head, second-guessing myself and everybody else, and boy does this get very tiring.

But in a strange way, for me, learning to live in reality was quite comforting after a while. I did not have to hide from myself and others anymore. I did not have to be that other person anymore, I did not have to be the good child anymore. I now had choices; they may not have been great choices, but they were choices.

When we live in the Red Zone over a prolonged period of time, we have no choices, because everything we do is about survival, and I would have impulsively done anything to survive. I reacted to everybody and everything automatically, and never realized how illogical it all was.

Through this program I came to realize that sadness, hurt, fear, etc. were a normal part of human existence. In fact, what was not normal was trying to escape from these feelings. It was the behaviors and the responses that I learned to escape from these feelings that were doing the damage. In this way these awful feelings stay with us forever. When we learn to accept that they are a normal part of our human existence and just allow them to be, they dissolve over time.

One really big learning I had in this Act was that feeling desperately sad in losing someone, and carrying that sadness over a prolonged period of time, was not helpful for me. Sadness was not the problem; my relationship with sadness was the problem, and it was holding me back.

I learned to focus on my relationship with sadness rather than the sadness. This takes time, but then again time is something we have plenty of.

One funny thing that I tapped into while trying to understand this Act in relation to myself, was that it tapped into something that my grandmother told me a long time ago. It was really ironic for me, who was addicted to being a good child. She said, "People who constantly try to do good all of the time, generally do more bad than good, both to themselves and others". There was wisdom personified for you.

I believe Paddy was so right in this Act when he said, and I quote, "I will begin to accept the unlivable, the unmanageable, the unhappiness of my life. I have confused through no fault of my own, the difference between reality and suffering, and made them different things. Reality and goodness, I don't know the difference so I objectify goodness, and this is a waste of time".

9

"BECOMING SUFFICIENTLY UNWELL YOU WILL FEEL COMPELLED TO DO SOMETHING ABOUT IT, BECAUSE YOU HAVE BEGUN TO REALIZE THAT THE PROBLEM IS IN YOU."

Having gotten this far, I have discovered that I am not the same person I was when I started at Act One. I am sure this is because I have a lot more information, which is helping me to understand myself a little bit more.

For me personally, this dawning of awareness as I called it began to offer the first chink of light that helped me to see that I could be okay. It is only when we start to feel well (even just a little bit) that we begin to realize how unwell we had become, and having tasted just a little bit of wellness, we want more of it.

There is no quick rush to wellness, I might add. There is no magic cure or quick fix.

Key to me understanding this Act was when I learned that the problem was not me, but that the problem was in me. This key information was vital for me because I went through all my life believing that I was the problem because of what had happened to me, and spent my whole life reacting to life and life's events. It was in reacting all the time that I made many mistakes and did lots of wrong things.

I was now becoming aware that the problem was in me because my programming was faulty and my beliefs were faulty. In many ways it was like a virus within me that completely skewed my view of both myself and the world around me.

This Act taught me that by acting I could configure this programming to a more positive and balanced setting. In my mind I was changing the polarity from a negative to a positive energy, and this was how I could turn things around.

At this point it was not necessary to know how to go about achieving this; the most important thing was that I was beginning to accept that the problem was in me and there was most definitely something I could do about it.

THIS FOR ME WAS THE BEGINNING OF EMPOWERMENT.

10

"YOU DECIDE TO ACT, TAKE RESPONSIBILITY FOR YOUR OWN LIFE. THIS WILL EMPOWER YOU AS YOU PARADOXICALLY REALIZE THAT POWERLESSNESS, WHETHER IT IS PEOPLE, EVENTS OR SITUATIONS, LEADS YOU TO AN ACCEPTANCE WHICH LEADS YOU TO SELF-EMPOWERMENT AND PEACE OF MIND."

There is a very old saying that goes:
"IT IS FROM SMALL ACORNS THAT GREAT OAK TREES GROW".

One of the things that I struggled with in this Act was that I wanted to change everything in the first few weeks. It can feel really good when we get that first slice of wellness, and we want more of it. But I had to remember that, up to now, every time I got something, I always wanted more. Much wants more was really appropriate for me, and once I got a small little bit of this wellness, I could not get enough of it.

However, after about two months I began to feel really anxious and crestfallen, as I was slowly creeping back into old ways of thinking, behaving and reacting.

What was the problem?

I wanted it all too quickly.

I had to stop and take stock of where I was and try to become aware of what the problem was.

One evening I was going through a box of some of my mother's old souvenirs and memory cards, when I came across a copy of the serenity prayer. My mother would have picked it up at one of her Al-

Anon meetings, which she attended periodically during her brief times of lucidity. I came across this prayer on many occasions over the years, but always tended to dismiss it as I saw it as something holy or religious and always felt that it did not do my mother much good anyway!

"God, grant me the serenity to accept the things I cannot change,

The courage to change the things I can, and the wisdom to know the difference".

Because, through this program, I was now looking at the word "God" and "Religion" differently, I could see that this was a very wise saying, and written by a very wise sage, which could be helpful to anybody in any situation, regardless of their beliefs.

The first learning I received was that I was trying to be a great oak tree, before I had ever even learned how to be an acorn.

The good thing was that I had decided to act, and try to change, but the problem was I had not fully realized what it was I was trying to change in the first place.

The acorn had to grow first. It had to be nurtured and understood, and only then would it become another acorn. I worked slowly, honestly and diligently to create all of these acorns one acorn at a time, without ever even thinking about the oak tree.

Then, all of a sudden, I woke up one morning and there was this great big oak tree. To this day I am not fully sure where it came from, but I do know that the day I decided to act, I planted the first seed.

When I decided to act, I decided I was going to change something, either myself or my perceptions. To do this I needed to decide what I could change and what I could not change.

I will give more insight into how I achieved all of this in the "Sixteen Key Actions" section of this program, but the key truth I took from this Act was:

I am powerless over other people, events, or situations, but I can change how I am in them, one step at a time, and by doing this I become empowered.

THAT IS A TRUTH AND A FACT.

11

"YOU HAVE COME TO THE REALIZATION THAT YOU CANNOT CHANGE ANYBODY ELSE. YOU WILL STOP RUMINATING AND LIVING IN YOUR HEAD, AND INSTEAD LIVE IN REALITY. NO LONGER THINKING ABOUT HOW THINGS SHOULD BE, BUT ACCEPTING HOW THINGS ARE.......... IN REALITY."

I would never in my wildest dreams have imagined that I had so little belief in myself, undervalued myself so much, and felt so unlovable, worthless and unacceptable. And in the depths of all that despair and faulty programming, I genuinely felt that other people looked at me that way as well.

To come to the realization that I could not change anybody else just so they would like me was really difficult for me. But we must remember that I had spent my life on a drug of approval, acceptance, and appreciation, and it was the only way I knew how to be in the world.

I know to the person looking in from the outside this must seem totally irrational and illogical, and it is. But for me this was my reality. I know now this was not reality, it was a fantasy. I was constantly living in my head all the time, in an imaginary world that had nothing to do with reality. People were never going to change, or perhaps better said, "I am not going to change them", and this then for me is a consolidation of Act Ten.

They are never going to change, because the truth is I can never change anybody, nor should I want to.

Paradoxically, I began to discover that the more I practiced change, and as I changed, other people in my surroundings began to change as well. Some for the good, and some not for the good. This is something that you just need to be aware of, but do not focus too much on it.

During this Act I really began to form a much clearer image of the continuum which I spoke about in Act Seven, which runs from the front of the Blue Zone to the back of the Red Zone.

Anytime I would find myself living in my head, and creating narratives and perceptions about other people and situations, I would recognize that I was on the wrong end of the continuum. A simple thing like a breath, just to re-center myself on the continuum, was very helpful.

As I keep pointing out, at this stage of the program you are still just creating awareness; it is not about getting it right. For me it was very helpful not to adapt a right or wrong mindset.

It is just all about learning, allowing ourselves to be imperfect. Making the mistakes, learning something from them, not beating ourselves up, remembering we are human.

Learn to live in reality and remember that once we have made a start, things will never be as bad again. It might feel that they're bad or even worse, but they're just feelings, they cannot hurt us. Always remember at this point that the behaviors and attachments that we learned through our programming to escape bad feelings are what are making us sick.

We are learning about these behaviors and attachments now. Continue this, keep working from the inside out, and keep making the necessary changes one step at a time.

Once we keep doing this with humility and honesty, I can almost guarantee you one "self-evident truth":

IT DOES GET BETTER.

This is not some illusional guarantee, this is based on the pure science of what we now know.

FEELINGS AND EMOTIONS ARE JUST ENERGIES MOVING IN THE BODY. ONCE we UNDERSTAND THEM, RESPECT THEM, BREATHE WITH THEM, AND ALLOW

THEM TO BREATHE, THEY WILL DISSOLVE AND FIND BALANCE. IT'S PHYSICS.
   JUST KEEP GOING ONE STEP AT A TIME.

12
"YOU HAVE COME TO THE REALIZATION THAT IT IS YOU WHO MUST CHANGE."

I have spent a lifetime living in fear and never realizing it. It was fear that was driving me all along.

The fear of not being good enough.

The fear that people might know that we were poor, that I was a dirty little abused unlovable boy, that people would know my mother was in the "Mental", that people might know my father was an alcoholic.

The fear that people might know who I really was.

Essentially, I always acted out of fear.

I always thought that when people looked at me, they saw me as I saw myself. Worthless, valueless, full of loathing, and that I could never feel peace or contentment until I could change people's perception of me.

How illogical was that?

Throughout the last couple of Acts and particularly in this Act, I really began to realize the truth. This was not me. These feelings did not stem from me, but from my programming, and there was a gap between myself, my programming, and who I really was.

Now, because I was starting to come into awareness just a little bit, and had decided to take responsibility to act and to begin the process of change, I could ask myself:

Why do I experience this inhumane view of myself?

Why do I beat myself up all the time?

Why do I constantly care what other people think of me?

It is not that I would not have tried to change before; I have, many times indeed. I must have a thousand self-help books, all lovely in their own way, but I always eventually found them to be patronizing and condescending.

That is not to say I vilify these books, because I don't, and I am sure that many people find them helpful. For me, it was the language I found very difficult to grasp and act on.

"You are one of God's angels, you deserve to be loved."

"The sky is your limit, you can be anything you want to be."

"Love yourself and the world will be yours."

They all sounded so good in the moment that I was reading them. But for me they were just aspirational and had no grounding in my reality. I do not think that people realize how difficult it is to "love yourself" when you have spent an entire life hating yourself.

If I were to get a Euro for every time somebody told me I just had to learn to "live in the present moment" and all would be well, I would be worth a fortune. I did not understand what "living in the present moment" actually meant, so how then could I suddenly wake up one morning and start doing it?

As Paddy Rafter said in his program, "It is like someone trying to teach me algebra, but I do not know what numbers are". It is impossible.

Eventually I did learn to live in the present moment, but that took time. And remember as you are doing these Acts that time is something that we have plenty of, so take our time.

The only thing that is important at this moment and time is that we have made a start, and that we are going to endeavor to keep going.

I began to see that I could change, that it was possible, that it was not slogans on a wall, or nice sayings in a book, or other people telling me what I should do; but that ultimately it would be me making a decision to try to understand these bad feelings and thoughts, and beginning to examine them for what they really were.

Very slowly and incrementally over time, I examined my thoughts and feelings, and I learned two great truths that were to help me significantly as I progressed on this program.

"It really does not matter what other people think of me. It only matters what I think of me."

"What other people think of me is their concern; do not make it my concern."

If we can embrace these great truths, we will never have to look back in fear again.

13

"WORKING A PROGRAM OF SELF-KNOWLEDGE AND SELF-EXAMINATION YOU ACCEPT WHO YOU ARE, GOOD AND BAD."

I found this Act really challenging. Self-knowledge and self-examination is very slow and difficult, but necessary things for us to undertake. I had spent my life running away from me, and I most certainly did not want to start looking at myself right now.

Why?

Primarily I was afraid of how bad I actually was.

Being challenged to look at the wrongs I had done, the embarrassments, the failures, the letting people down—why would I want to look at these?

The answer? Because I had to.

The twelve previous Acts have led me to this Act, and I now know that it was not my fault that these things happened. It was because of my addiction to the drug of approval and appreciation. But having arrived here and knowing what I now know, if I continue to act in the same way, the consequences will now be my fault, because I am aware and I am beginning to try to separate my present actions from my past programming.

I had to learn to accept myself, both good and bad. One of the things I did learn in this Act was that my intentions were always good. I genuinely wanted to fix people and make the world a better place. I just got hopelessly lost in the addictive process of trying to achieve that.

I slowly began to realize, "You know what, I was not all that bad", but the ability to self-reflect in any meaningful way had been lost to me. Working through this program began to open a door for me to be able to see "that" which was always hidden to me.

And what was that "that", one might ask?

That I was not all bad. That deep inside there was a child who was lost, hurting, and crying in the dark.

It was up to me to take that hurt child by the hand and bring him out of the darkness, with patience and understanding, which would in time lead to reconciliation.

This is the one Act where we can really have a setback. We have been gaining a little confidence, and feeling a little better about ourself as we begin the slow process of change, and now we have to face the challenge of having to look at the difficulties that our addictive behaviors may have caused us, and in particular, other people in our life.

There can be a tendency to want to run off and fix all the harms we might have perpetrated on our addictive journey. Now is not the time, because we are not ready yet. Maybe in the future we will be able to do that, but not now.

We are not ready for that now. We first have to build up our own self-confidence through self-examination, the learning of knowledge and more understanding. I do not mean that in a narcissistic way (it's all about my feelings), but I mean it in a more balanced way. The more that we learn about ourself, the more we will learn about other people and the world around us, which over time will put us in a much better position to handle people's different reactions to us and accept them for where they are coming from.

By doing this with diligence and patience we will learn:
TO ACCEPT WHO YOU ARE, GOOD AND BAD.

14

"THEN YOU WILL WAKE UP AND BECOME AWARE. BY BECOMING AWARE YOU CAN SEE ALL THINGS AS THEY REALLY ARE. SEE YOURSELF AND YOUR RIGHT TO EXIST. YOU WILL SEE THE NATURE OF ALL THINGS."

This Act is really where, for the first time, I began to see things as they were and not as the way I wanted to see them. I was this very fragile, very fractured child, adolescent, and adult who wanted the world to be a happy place. Who wanted to fix people and things and who trusted everybody and everything.

Carl Jung wrote about "our shadow", our dark side, our capacity for evil. I now know that this darkness is in every one of us, and being aware of it is essential for a balanced and peaceful view of self and the world. After all, if I never walked in the darkness, how could I ever appreciate the light?

I would be very much in concurrence with Paddy Rafter, where in this Act he says:

"We have become savages, we have become ignorant. We have not evolved. We have evolved technologically, but in every other sense we have devolved (regressed). It is almost like our evolution is going backwards completely out of sync and out of balance with the world around us".

The reason that I concur is because as I was working through this program and was beginning to feel a little better about myself, a little bit more aware, and gaining a sense of freedom, I became aware that I needed to gain a greater understanding of this newfound freedom and how to act appropriately within it.

I learned very quickly that freedom is not freedom just for the sake of it; it has to be treated with great responsibility. Freedom does not give us the license to say or do what we want, when we want. If that was the case, we would have anarchy.

When we have been hurt in life, we can quite often feel the need to stand up on the rooftops and tell everybody what has happened to us and also name the person or persons who have perpetrated our hurt and trauma. I understand this fully. But we must also understand that everybody has the right to due process, and everybody is innocent until proven guilty. If this does not happen the world would descend into the law of the jungle, and that would not be in anybody's best interest.

Unfortunately, in today's society people's names are just put out into the public domain, to be tried and executed on social media, gossip shows, etc., all in the name of entertainment and ratings, with no due process, no awareness of how people's lives and the lives of their families and communities can be changed forevermore (and sometimes these people are completely innocent).

That is not to say that people should not be held accountable for their actions; of course they should, but this is not the way. This is no different to how things were done many years ago, where people were stoned at the stockades, burned at the stakes, put into the great amphitheaters to survive against the gladiators, all with no trial, no due process. Everything was decided in the public domain, with a thumbs up or a thumbs down.

Technology has made our environment very corrosive as the whole world is judging us now, and nobody knows the truth or the facts. They just think they do because they heard it or read it somewhere.

I believe this is what Paddy Rafter is speaking about when he says "we have regressed".

This Act has really taught me that becoming aware comes with a warning notice. In the recorded history of humanity, any time peoples and nations got their freedom from years of oppression, almost in every case a civil war ensued, as people had not learned appropriately how to deal with the years of suppressed hurts and traumas that had been inflicted upon them.

We individual humans are no different. When we begin to come into awareness, and we start to access the hurts which all of us have endured at some point and are buried deep in our Red Zone, we have to know how to handle them appropriately. And we don't know, because nobody ever taught us. Now what is happening is that people are using social media to weaponize that part of themselves that they do not understand. This is only succeeding in bringing out the very worst parts of ourselves as we access what Carl Jung called "our shadow", which is really that part of ourselves that we disown, and when we do not have awareness of this, we look to transfer our awful feelings onto others.

Freedom from oppression of any kind must be treated with the utmost respect, thoughtfulness and understanding, otherwise we just end up inflicting onto others what we believe they have inflicted onto us. This creates an ugly, hurt, angry, conflictual society.

This is my hurt, my trauma, my story, and nobody has the right to use my story to champion their own causes. I will understand it, nurture it, own it, and then in my own time, with awareness, I will act accordingly and appropriately.

THIS IS FREEDOM. THIS IS AWARENESS.

15

"THROUGH KNOWLEDGE AND AWARENESS YOU WILL DISCERN THAT THERE IS A POWER GREATER THAN YOU."

It was back in Act Three that I began to examine, for the first time, what a power greater than me actually means and in a different context to the way I would have understood it heretofore.

It is only now as I have arrived at Act Fifteen, even though I have worked through from Act Three up to now, that I really get what this means.

The idea of a power greater than me is really that I can now understand the force of the energy of the universe, the energy of existence.

Without even consciously thinking about it in the previous Acts, as I began to incrementally get well and feel the energy change within me, I figured out that the energy of living is the energy of life.

As my energy changed and became more positive in its output, the energy of life around me was changing in a positive way also. I could begin to feel it, touch it, and see it. I didn't need some interlocutors who had been put in place to explain it to me, to be the "middleman" to connect me to this "named God", this "higher power" who manipulated me.

You do not have to go look for this energy, because it is present all around us. this comes in love for ourself and the world around us. In goodness and kindness to ourself and the world around us.

It is to help others altruistically where there is no benefit to you. This is all around us, this energy, since time began. This is the one thing we cannot survive without, this has never changed. What has changed is our perception of this "higher power", particularly in the past ten thousand to twelve thousand years, mainly through manipulation for control.

I never knew it was there; how could I? When we are really sick, we do not live in the real world. I lived in another world, a world of unreality.

All I have to do is experience it, this energy of existence, this "God" that has been there before humans ever came on the planet. This is indisputable, this is true.

16
"YOU WILL HAVE A GOD, NOT OF YOUR OWN IMAGE, BUT OF REALITY."

I grew up as a Roman Catholic, and dutifully and diligently practiced the teachings of the church and read the Bible as much as Catholics were encouraged to. In hindsight my actions were more out of fear than any feelings of great nurture and love. But I suppose that is the way it was, and I knew no different.

It was indoctrinated into me, that there was only one "God" and to believe in any other "false god" was a "sin", which would bring upon us punishment and the "wrath of God". Any sort of examination was most definitely not encouraged. "God the Almighty" was the "Higher Power" and indeed the only power. Out of pure habit we became normalized into seeing the world this way.

It was only when I went to the Middle East for the first time as a young soldier with a United Nations peacekeeping mission that I began to question these teachings for the first time.

The area of the Middle East I was working in at the time was a mainly Muslim conclave, whom I discovered had a completely different God to the one I grew up with. His name was Allah and he was the only God. But yet I had been told that the Christian God was the only God and that all the others were "false".

The Nepalese soldiers who we worked with were a mixture of

Hindu and Buddhist. The Hindus worship thirty-three million gods. The Buddhists had no belief in a personal God, but followed the path of the Buddha Siddhartha Gautama who went on a quest for enlightenment around the sixth century BC.

As far as I could see, God was anything you wanted it to be, or any image you wanted it to be. They were images created by people at moments of time. In a lot of cases, they are false gods, an image we have in our head that we create, or that somebody else created for us.

These are just names that people put on something that we have always known has been there for millions of years, this higher power, this obvious reality that there is a power greater than ourselves.

In reality there is only one God, there only has ever been one God, for millions and millions of years; it's existence, it's reality. This is indisputable. I came to this conclusion, not because it is a conclusion, but because it is an inescapable fact.

This new awareness and understanding of the higher power which I was receiving through my understanding of this program, for me personally was a game changer. It did not require me to blindly follow rules, to pay homage to a middle man, to get confused by mixed messages and manipulations. It just allowed me to be, to be at peace with something I did not have to name. This gave me awareness, and with awareness came enlightenment. When I got enlightenment, for the very first time I could see, I could feel, I could trust. I knew it was something that was ever-present, but it was up to me to tap into it, to plug into that eternal source of energy that has always been there.

All of this eventually brings balance and trust. We know we would never intentionally do anybody a wrong or an injustice. We want to be well, but we want everybody else to be well also. There is no "us and them", no divisions, no divisiveness of different religions and ideologies.

For me now, this is simply the way it always has been throughout almost our entire history. Groups of hunter-gatherers coming together and working together, as one, to cherish and give thanksgiving to this wonderful world we have been given, and to pass it on in the same wonderful way, if not better, to the many generations to come.

Having now completed the first sixteen Acts, I can see the great value they are. How they can help other people.

They offer unbelievable clarity, logic and progression, and I can see why they are the way they are.

These sixteen Acts on their own are revelatory, because they make us grow if we work them. The beauty of their simplicity and logical progression is that understanding them makes you understand yourself.

Following these Acts so far has profoundly affected me. I can see that this could work for you or anybody.

I never had any of the most recognized addictions like alcohol, drugs, gambling, sex, etc., and yet as I worked this program, I saw how strongly addicted I was.

I now fully understand what Paddy Rafter meant when he said, "Each one of us is addicted to something". We all need help, and this program has been an unbelievable help to me.

THE LAYMAN'S GUIDE TO THE "SIXTEEN FALSE BELIEFS"

I
"YOU CANNOT BE HAPPY WITHOUT THE THINGS THAT YOU ARE ATTACHED TO AND THAT YOU BELIEVE TO BE ALL-IMPORTANT."

FALSE

Essentially every one of us as humans just wants to be happy, to feel that we belong, and to have a sense of purpose and meaning in our lives. I think that is pretty much basic for all of us; it certainly was for me anyway.

Since the Industrial Revolution, society has been driving forward, at an ever-increasing pace within the model of bigger, faster, stronger. Every generation wanted the next generation to be better off than they were, and each upcoming generation wanted to be better off than the generation that went before them. I am not saying that there is anything inherently wrong with this—there isn't, because ambition is important—but it must be paired with awareness.

Has it honestly made us any happier?

When we do not have awareness, we can so easily be manipulated. The powerful marketing forces of the capitalist consumer model tells us that we have never been "better off". We have bigger houses and bigger cars, travelling anywhere in the world is so accessible for most people now, we are more educated, we have made huge advances in science and medicine, technology is making our lives so much more convenient. I think it is easy to see why the marketers' claims might be true and that we do indeed appear to be happier. There are millions of books which will tell you that we have never been happier.

But are we?

Or are we just pretending to be happy, as that is the way the world expects us to be now.

I was one of those people who believed that more education, more holidays, bigger house, bigger car, more belongings, and nicer clothes would make me happier. They did not. I confused momentary thrills, short bursts of excitement, and the chase for the next thing that I could attach myself to, with happiness. And guess what? They did not make me any happier; they made me more unhappy, but I had been sucked into a model that taught me this:

"My wants are more important than my needs."

I might want all of these things, but the truth (and this Act challenged me to explore this) was: did I need them? And the answer most definitely was NO.

Modern life has become a competition, and humans are just commodities to be measured and put on a matrix someplace. Life now is about how we look, and not how we feel. All we are doing is creating a facade and papering over the cracks. It is a fantasy world called pretend, where most people live their lives in the alternate world of social media, where everybody "appears to be happy".

It could not be more obvious that the world has never been unhappier. We seem to be stuck in crisis mode all the time. We have never been sicker; medicine may be getting better, but if we are getting sicker that model is not sustainable. In trying to keep up with the capitalistic consumer model there has never been so much financial frailty within families. Look at the level of human conflict, judgement, angst, anger, anxiety and addictions that exist within all levels of society now.

I discovered that my needs were actually very easily met, for I needed very little. I have now learned through this Act, how to become aware and how to look after my own needs.

I might want all of these things (and that is ok) but when I honestly ask myself if I need them in order to be happy? Most definitely not.

All of these attachments are ways of trying to seek approval and appreciation, a way of finding belonging in an increasingly anxious world, because the truth is we do not feel that we belong within ourselves anymore, and we do not know how to remedy this. You will know from reading this book that when anxiety increases in humans, families and society, we become more susceptible to manipulation by the powerful marketing forces that want us to believe that we need their attachments to be happy.

But remember, the more anxious we become, the more we retreat to our Red Zone. Now our thinking and behaviors will become more irrational, illogical, reckless and self-centered. The paradox now is that we will believe we need more of these attachments to be happy, to belong, and so we get stuck in the cycle of anxiety. There is only one ending when this happens: even more unhappiness.

There is a great irony here within this model of "bigger, faster, stronger", for it now appears that through lack of awareness, greed and an insatiable desire to accumulate attachments, the present generation are set to be worse off than all previous generations. They have been saddled with a huge debt crisis, a world that is disintegrating through a manmade climate crisis, and levels of fear, anxiety, and sickness of both mind and body that are unprecedented in our recorded history.

This ideology of "bigger, faster, stronger" has not worked for society.

So let us correct the falsehood that you have been programmed with, and reprogram it to read:

"You CAN be happy without the things that you are attached to and that you believe to be all important".

The great learning, I received in this Act was that I could not think my way or buy my way to happiness. The way to happiness was to allow myself to feel my way into the organic happiness within. Through this gut and instinctual journey of learning how to belong to me, I organically, over time, was incrementally arriving to the happiness within. It takes time, it takes patience, it takes understanding, but persevere; we will get there.

❦ 2 ❧
"YOU BELIEVE HAPPINESS IS IN THE FUTURE: WHEN YOU GET A NEW HOUSE, CAREER OR RELATIONSHIP, FAME OR WEALTH".

FALSE
Although Acts One and Two are both very similar, this Act really resonated with me. To me, happiness was always something that I was striving for, and it was out there in the future once I had achieved everything I desired. I just had to get out there and find it.

This of course meant that in my thinking I was always somewhere in the future, and ironically at the same time I was running from my past. And of course, if you are constantly worrying about the future, and full of fear about the past, well then you will never enjoy or be in the present.

I never realized that the constant striving to be better, to be somebody that everybody would look up to, and wanting people to see that I was somebody who could make a difference, was making me more anxious by the day.

Without awareness, I did not realize that the more anxious I was getting, the more I was retreating to live in the Red Zone of my brain.

The more I lived in the Red Zone, the more I was reconnecting to the unprocessed stored memories which I was running away from in the first place. This in turn made me even more anxious (uneasy), which now meant that I became even more attached to my faulty programming that constantly told me that I needed all of these attachments to be happy.

Without even realizing it, I was retreating even deeper into the Red Zone, which saw me disconnecting even further from the Blue Zone of my brain. Now my thinking became even more irrational, and my behavior became even more reckless. This caused me to lose touch with reality, and over time I learned to live in an alternative, fantasy world.

I became even more invested in my journey of achieving happiness. I was always full of anxiety, full of fear, but the truth is I was never going to be happy if I was waiting for something or somebody out there to make me happy.

What we really need to understand here is that the more we live in the Red Zone, the more messages are sent to all of the cells in the human organism to say that danger is imminent. The cells respond with equal fervor, everything becomes unbalanced, and eventually all the anxiety (unease) becomes the disease and we get sick. A lot of this is through our faulty thinking that truly believes:

"We will find happiness in the future: when we get a new house, career or relationship, fame or wealth".

You won't. I didn't.

More and more as I was going through this program, I was really enhancing my scientific and cognitive education about the brain by learning to be more present in my gut. Over time, I instinctively began to trust that I would find happiness in an organic way.

3

"YOU FEEL ANGER, RESENTMENT, FEAR, DISAPPOINTMENT, AND SHAME, AND THESE JUSTIFY YOUR BEHAVIORS. YOU ARE YOUR FEELINGS."

False

"It is not my fault; sure, I was born this way."

This is what I truly believed and thought for most of my life. This program has allowed me to have a greater understanding of the consequences of thinking this way.

One of the difficulties with this way of thinking and believing is that we can easily justify our decision-making and our behaviors, and not feel that we have to take any responsibility for the consequences.

This is based on a faulty belief system which is telling us that we are these feelings. The following statements are examples of this mindset.

"I grew up in a dysfunctional family."

"I am and always will be a victim."

"That feeling of shame is because I grew up in a poor, socially deprived background, and that is the reason I am the way that I am. There is nothing I can do about it anyway."

"Sure, what can I do, it is in the genes." I could go on and on.

These are false beliefs that are part of our programming, and they feed the narratives and stories that we are creating in our own head. This is purely because we cannot cope with the anxiety (unease) that is created by our faulty thinking, which is continually sending messages down the body, to prepare for danger (and most of the time there is no danger, it is just that our thinking is telling us there is). All our energies are now being constantly disrupted and relocated for the "fight, flight, freeze" survival response, and this creates a really bad feeling inside our head and our body.

This is a short-term survival response that is instinctive in every one of us through the course of our evolution, which enables us to act and behave in a certain way to deal with real danger (tiger in the savanna).

While this survival response continues, we keep tapping into our deep feelings of insecurity, and our body stays stuck in this "bad feeling" mode.

The only thing that we have to do at this moment in time is to begin to become aware and start to recognize this false belief that tells us, "You are your feelings".

We most definitely are not.

For now, all we have to do is begin to open our mind to the fact that things might not be the way we thought they were.

As each Act was coming and going, I was becoming more aware of learning to sit with and experience the feelings in my body, and not just cognitively live with the thoughts in my head as I would have heretofore. More and more, over time I was beginning to instinctively trust that if I just stayed with this program and its teachings, I would be okay.

❦ 4 ❦
"YOU FEEL ANGER, DISAPPOINTMENT, RESENTMENT, FEAR, SHAME, ETC., BECAUSE OF WHAT SOMEONE ELSE SAID OR DID TO YOU, AND THIS JUSTIFIES YOUR BEHAVIOR."

FALSE

This Act helped me to see that I have spent almost an entire lifetime believing that:

I had to prove to people that I was not the person they thought I was, and that I would show them, and that I was only behaving in a certain way because of what happened to me.

I genuinely believed that everything about my behavior was because of what other people did to me, and it drove me along to try to right all the wrongs and injustices of the world. This in turn allowed me to justify my actions and behaviors. But how would I have known any better? It was the only way I knew in my quest to escape and to survive these deeply repressed feelings of fear, shame, guilt, hurt, etc.

But what else would I believe? I did not realize that it was my programming that led me to believe that my behavior was justified in the first place. My programming entitled me to behave in this way; it was the nature of the human condition, the nature of reality.

I now know that this is not true. It is not reality, so I had to learn to begin to separate things in my mind.

Firstly, I have learned that yes, bad things have happened to me in my life. That is irrefutable. That is true. There is no denying it.

Secondly, I learned that yes, the awful feelings that I experienced because of these bad things were real and completely overwhelmed me. That is irrefutable. That is true. There is no denying it.

Thirdly, I learned that yes, because I did not know what to do with these horrendous bad feelings, I buried them deep into my Red Zone and I subconsciously created maladaptive behaviors to help me escape and avoid these overwhelming sensations. It was these learned maladaptive behaviors that ultimately formed my programming.

It was these maladaptive behaviors, which were part of my programming, that were making me sick. It was not the events, not the people. I cannot do anything about what happened. I cannot do anything about what other people say or do. But I did learn to own my own feelings; they are mine, they are real, and if I trust my gut they will not hurt me anymore.

It was the maladaptive behaviors and their consequences that were hurting both myself and other people around me.

There was something that I could do to understand my maladaptive behaviors and their consequences. Take ownership of them and learn to take personal responsibility for them.

By doing this consistently over time, I would put myself in a position to rewrite my programming.

What I did not realize, of course, was that the more anxious I became, the more I retreated into my Red Zone. The more I retreated into my Red Zone, the more I was reconnecting to the deeply repressed emotions that I was trying to escape from in the first place, and the more anxious and overwhelmed I became. As the anxiety increased, so too did the maladaptive behaviors and their consequences, because I now needed to work even harder to escape these awful feelings which were not getting any better.

Just like in the previous Acts, I was incrementally learning that although I had a great grasp of the science behind my work, enhancing my gut and instinctual knowing would prove invaluable to me on my journey to recovery.

Through this Act I learned to change, so I know that you can also.

❧ 5 ❧
"IN ORDER TO CEASE YOUR MALADAPTIVE BEHAVIORS AND ADDICTIONS YOU MUST CONSTANTLY IDENTIFY WITH OTHERS WHO HAVE DONE SO, INSTEAD OF EMULATING WHAT THEY HAVE DONE TO DATE."

FALSE

Many years ago, when I was a teenager, I used to attend Al-a-teen meetings. These were support groups for children who were affected by somebody drinking within the family.

In my early adult years, I used to attend ACOA meetings. These were support groups for adults who grew up in alcoholic homes, and as a result were still experiencing difficulties in their own lives, even though they might not be drinking or using.

In very recent times I have been attending a support group for Adult Survivors of Sexual Abuse.

The first thing I should say is that these support groups are very helpful and beneficial for anybody who attends, and can offer a sense of belonging and an often much needed network of support.

I would not say I was a regular attendee at these groups, but tended to dip in and out as required because something, for some reason or another, never seemed to sit right with me, even though I could never put a name on what I was sensing or experiencing at that time.

Whether it was some of the participants within the groups, or the facilitator on occasion, I am not quite sure. That is not to say that the groups were not beneficial; of course they were, and for certain a lot of people have gotten a lot of help from these groups. However, for me something was not quite right, so I did not attend as much as maybe I would have needed to and liked to.

It was only when I came to this Act that for the first time, I got an insight into what I was experiencing and why.

The word you actually hear more than any other word at these meetings, is the word "identify".

I would attend a meeting and listen to the testament of the speaker, and in almost all cases the next person to speak would start with, "I can identify with the last speaker". Then when my turn came to speak, I immediately started with, "I can identify with what the last speaker said". At the very early stages of these meetings this was a good thing, as it made you realize that you were not alone and that everybody else had problems and similar experiences as well.

Looking back now I can see that the same people tended to frequent these meetings, constantly identifying with others, but never appearing to be changing themselves.

I now started to see why I struggled with these meetings. I was the ultimate identifier; I spent most of my life identifying and hiding in other people's pain, in order to escape my own pain.

Another problem was that I could often over-identify and believe that their story was much more devastating than mine. This had the effect of me minimizing my own difficulties and being cross with myself, and the upshot was I never did anything to help myself, which made me feel even more unworthy.

The other side of that coin was when other people's problems seemed not as bad as mine. I would end up judging them and despising them (in my head), which did not really help to cultivate compassion and empathy for others. It was almost like a sense of righteousness, and it did not lead to wellness.

I can now see, through this Act, that I spent a lifetime identifying it in others but never (until recently) got around to changing it in myself.

How many of us (a good many, I would imagine) are really good at preaching and giving advice to others about how they should be living their lives, but have no idea how to apply the same advice to manage their own life?

This idea that you have to identify all the time is false. Constant identification with other people's pain keeps you living in the Red Zone, where you constantly stay connected to and identifying with your own suppressed feelings that you have no idea how to deal with.

I know this for a fact because that was me, constantly identifying and hiding in other people's stories to escape my own.

In the short term it is good to be able to identify with others, but then we must make the necessary changes within ourselves.

❧ 6 ☙
"YOU MUST CEASE YOUR MALADAPTIVE BEHAVIORS AND ADDICTIONS ON THE INSTIGATION OF OTHERS."

F ALSE
I have come across many people in my working life, including in my own family, who ended up in rehab programs (often very expensive ones), psychiatric institutions, and various forms of counselling and therapies, as a result of outside interventions.

I have taken part in many of these interventions myself, both as a facilitator and as a family member.

The idea and thinking around these interventions are that first, a group of concerned people would come together over a period of time to discuss their concerns over the addiction and/or maladaptive behaviors of somebody they all know. Next, they would discuss whether there was anything they could do to try and shine a spotlight on this loved one and their maladaptive behaviors. Ultimately, all of this is done with a view to get the addict or the person who is unwell to see the reality of the consequences of their maladaptive behaviors.

The makeup of this intervention group would be concerned family members, a boss from work, concerned close friends, etc., and someone to facilitate.

The idea then is that a suitable time would be selected, where the addict or unwell person ends up sitting in a group (with no prior knowledge) and are confronted with their maladaptive behaviors and the damage these behaviors were doing to everybody else present. They are told they need to change immediately, or there will be consequences such as:

Losing their job,

A barring order from the home,

Withdrawal of friendships,

And various other consequences. The addict/unwell person is then given a couple of days to think about this, and then make a decision. If the deadline passes without the addict/unwell person conforming, well, then the consequences will kick in.

This is all established on a reality-based model that puts a mirror up in front of the addict/unwell person, and they are presented with the reality of what the consequences of their maladaptive behaviors are having on everyone else in the room. The underlying principle is that if they are presented with the reality of their maladaptive behaviors, they will see the reality and want to do something to change.

How absurd and almost delusional is that? It shows a huge lack of awareness and understanding of how the human condition actually works, or does not work in the first place. The idea is that we are attempting to shame the person into making a change. And remember that we are confronting a person who is carrying deep issues of shame and guilt in the first place. It simply does not and could not work.

The idea is that if you present the addict (and remember we are all addicted, and are at some point on the continuum) with reality and its consequences, that they might see this reality and subsequently want to change. This is a truly false assumption, because although everybody on the outside can see the irrational behavior and its consequences, for the addict this is their reality. They have no capacity to differentiate, as they are working on faulty programming and this is their reality.

What tends to happen is that a compliant person will conform and agree to do something because they want to keep people happy, and will do anything to belong and to be liked. So, in the short term, they will comply, they will go to therapy, they will go into rehab, and in the short term will appear to be getting better. However, statistics will tell us that this is often a false recovery and often short-lived.

The reason for this short-lived recovery of course is that the reason for going for treatment was flawed in the first place. It was ever only about pleasing and keeping other people happy, and the confronted person just learned to play the game.

A really angry person will just storm out, and descend further into the hopeless pit that they are already trying to survive in.

If other people keep telling us that we "must" stop it is literally a waste of time. Not only does it not help, it has a zero effect as it is based on a false assumption.

The only way that we can get well is the day that we decide that we want to get well for ourselves, but the big problem is that due to our faulty programming, we believe that we are not worth getting well for.

But we are worth getting well for, and I know this to be true. That is why this program and these Acts were beneficial for me, because they educated me about myself, they gave me knowledge, understanding, awareness, and a journey into wellness that was incremental and at my own pace. And when I began to get well, I began to understand that the shame and the guilt that I was feeling were not real; they were manifestations of my programming, but they were not me. As I began to understand how I had arrived into this dark hole and began to make small changes one step at a time, these feelings dissipated.

We do not have to change everything at this point. It is not all-or-nothing, it is about becoming aware, and seeing the need to change from within ourselves, not because somebody else wants us to. By doing this we can become well. I know we can, because I did.

This program works, because it is coming from the inside out, from within us, purely because we want it.

7
"YOU WILL BE HAPPY IF YOU CHANGE OTHERS, OR IF THE PEOPLE CLOSEST TO YOU CHANGE."

FALSE
This is another false assumption that comes from our faulty programming.

I have spent an entire lifetime trying to change others, and hoping other people would change, which turned out to be a waste of time.

My head was forever full of thoughts like the following.

"If I could change my mother, she would not have to go to the 'Mental'."

"If I could stop my father's drinking, my mother would get better."

"If people liked me, I might feel better about myself."

"If I can change people's perception of me, they might see that I am a good boy."

"If only he changed."

"If only people would be different."

"If only that."

"If only."

"If."

We cannot change others, and it is a false belief based on our faulty programming to believe that we can.

We can only change ourselves. We cannot change what we are in, but we can change how we are in it.

Often when we begin to change, guess what? It can have the effect of other people changing around us.

8
"HAPPINESS IS IN THINGS, PEOPLE AND ASSUMPTIONS, AND THE WORLD OUTSIDE."

FALSE

As I was working my way through this particular Act and getting a greater understanding of things, I came to the conclusion that happiness and rainbows are very similar. They both offer a pot of gold when we get to the end of them.

A rainbow is a beautiful picture that we can see in the sky. However, if we go searching for it in order to get the pot of gold that allegedly sits at the end of it, we will never find it. The reason for this, of course, is that the rainbow is not really a thing and it does not exist in a particular place. It is an optical phenomenon that appears when sunlight and atmospheric conditions are just right—*and* if the viewer's position is just right to see it.

Is happiness any different? In the marketing world, happiness is being sold as the ultimate pot of gold at the end of the rainbow. We are very cleverly, both overtly and covertly, being manipulated to believe that events, people, and accumulations of things will ultimately make us happy. They won't, and to believe that they will is a false belief.

Happiness, just like the rainbow, is not really a thing that can be acquired, purely because happiness is not a thing.

Happiness is a state that exists within us, and because we live our lives so connected to the world outside of us, we very rarely get to that place deep inside of us where happiness exists.

Although happiness and the rainbow have many similarities, the one place where they are different is that while the rainbow is an optical phenomenon, happiness is real. But just like the rainbow, happiness can only be experienced when conditions are just right—and the viewer's position is just right.

So, let me make that simpler for you. Sunlight is awareness, so to experience happiness we must have awareness. Atmospheric conditions are the balance of mind and body, and if they are in balance, well then you will be in the right position to experience the feeling of happiness which is coming from deep within you.

Happiness is in the stillness, it is in the undoing, not the constant doing. It is the letting go of attachments and accumulations that have clouded our minds. It is in the stilling of the mind.

All of this, of course, takes time and patience, but it is most definitely achievable for each and every one of us.

At this point in time we just need to create a dialogue in our own head that tells us that happiness will not be achieved in things, possessions, people and the world outside of us. This is what deprogramming is all about; it is simply, through increased knowledge and awareness, using what I call self-talk therapy, and an enhanced awareness of gut and instinctual knowing to assist us to rewrite faulty programming. This takes time, but we will get there.

9
"IF I CHANGE EVERYTHING I HAVE, AND ACHIEVE EVERYTHING I WISH TO DO, I WILL BE HAPPY."

FALSE

This Act I can most certainly relate to. I spent my lifetime trying to change me, because I hated me and the way I constantly felt about myself. I genuinely felt that with this great ambition and desire to make the world and humanity a better place, I would achieve the ultimate nirvana of happiness. It did not work; it just made me unhappier.

I am not saying that they are not good traits to have, because they are, and if you wish to do those things because you feel that they will help other people, that is fine. But in the long term they did not help me, because without awareness they just made me feel worse over time. Of course, I got some fleeting glances of feeling good about myself, but they never lasted because it was not sustainable. You know the old saying "much wants more"? That was me. Every time I got a sniff of happiness, it would fade, and now I had to work even harder to get the next sniff, but it became more elusive.

The paradox is that the harder I was working to find happiness outside of myself, the further away I was travelling from the spot where happiness exists, inside of me.

I am not saying that we should not want to achieve anything we want, or help other people, or try to make a positive difference in the world. Of course, we should, but it must be done with awareness. If we are doing it just so we can be happy, well, then it is a waste of time, and we will never be happy.

The reason I do these things now is because with the help of this program I have come to the awareness that it is the right thing to do. I have learned not to give purely just to receive. If we can give to somebody, hopefully they will pass that goodness on to someone else, and they in turn pass it on to somebody else, and eventually over time the goodness comes back in ways that we could never have imagined.

❧ 10 ☙
"IF ALL MY DESIRES ARE FULFILLED AND ALL MY DREAMS COME TRUE THEN I WILL BE HAPPY."

FALSE

I must say that I had an ironic chuckle to myself when I read this Act. This one sentence summed up my entire life. If you read my testimony at the start of this book, you will know that I have been following the desires and dreams of my nine-year-old self for over fifty years. I was the hurt nine-year-old boy who dreamed incessantly about wanting to:

"Grow up and make a difference in the world",

"Be somebody",

"Fix everybody and make them all happy", and

"Grow up to be some sort of a superhero, so that everybody will love me".

Firstly, I should say that there is nothing inherently wrong with having dreams and desires. They are important, but they must be coupled with awareness and reality.

Without awareness, dreams become nightmares, and desires become toxic.

How many superstars of film, sport, and music have you read about who followed their dreams and desires of being superstars at their chosen sport or art, and although they achieved their desire or dream, we learned that they were lost in addictions of one kind or another, or became mentally or physically unwell?

Too many to say, I would suggest. When we do not have awareness and balance, and we are relentlessly driving forward to be the best and make real our dreams and desires, we are unknowingly living in our Red Zone. As the night follows the day, this is guaranteed to make us very sick, either in mind or body, or both. (Just like me, until I came across this program.)

People would often say to me that my parents and grandparents endured because they had a great faith in their God. In my parents' case this was not true, because it was a blind faith based on a false belief that God would look after them if they handed everything over to him.

The upshot of this was that they lived their life in denial, and never dealt with the difficulties that they could and should have been doing something about, because they believed that God was going to do it for them.

That is not to say that faith is not a good thing; it is, but it must be balanced with awareness.

In the same way, dreams and desires are a good thing, but without awareness they have the potential to destroy our lives and the lives of others.

This is a very difficult concept to get people to buy into, particularly in a market-driven world that constantly tells us that "if we follow our desires and dreams, we can be anything we want to be".

I have learned the hard way that we cannot be anything that we want to be. That is a fact, whether we like it or not. I would love to be a leading man in a Broadway musical, but guess what? I never will.

Why?

I can't sing.

So, in conclusion, we cannot be anything we desire or dream to be.

But what I can tell you, and what I have learned in this program, is that with balance and awareness and a greater level of gut and instinctual trust,

We can be happy.

We can make a difference in a positive way in our own life and in the lives of others.

We can be our best self.

❧ 11 ❧
"IF MY LOVE DEPENDS ON OTHERS AND I CLING TO THEM AND CONTROL THEM IN A CAGE OF LOVE, I WILL BE HAPPY."

FALSE

We all need to be a part of something, and each one of us has an innate desire to belong. We need to be able to give love, but also, we need to be able to receive love as well. If this goes out of balance, there will be problems.

The first question I should ask here is:

What is love?

This is a very difficult question to answer, as everybody will have a different interpretation of what love means to them. If we go and look at the different definitions in the different encyclopedias and dictionaries, we will get a mixed bag of meanings and interpretations.

As I am working my way through this program, and getting a much greater understanding of my own programming, I can see without doubt that I grew up with a very distorted view of love.

There was absolutely no showing of affection or love in our house growing up. That is not to say that my parents did not love us. I am sure that they did. The problem was that they had no way of expressing it, so we became starved of it through our perceptions.

I can see now, in my own life, how I believed that love was getting people to like me and constantly looking for approval and affection, sometimes with the most devastating consequences.

I wrote earlier on in this book about how I became my mother's confidant at times when she would become very unwell. No matter what I was doing, or whatever time of the day or night that my mother would call, I would drop everything just to go to her. I would spend hours listening to her tales of woe. She would tell me that I was so "good" and that I was the only one who "understood her" or who "cared enough". She would tell me that I was "special". I confused this with love and felt so blessed to have had this special relationship with my mother.

I now know, of course, that this was not love, but was my mother's deep sense of insecurity and possessiveness. My mother had no awareness or insight into how my life was being affected by her expectations that I would just drop everything to go to her when she called; and I did, as this was the only way I could feel that she loved me.

I truly believed that I was making my mother happier, and in turn I would be happier as well, because I was being a good son.

This was not love, the reality was that (unknowingly) both of us were trapped in a cage of possessiveness, control and dependency.

We can never make somebody else love us, despite what the powerful marketing of the capitalistic consumer model is telling us.

Love is not gifts and grand gestures on a continual basis to make them love us. To believe that almost borders on delusional, and is a manifestation of our faulty programming.

I have learned through this program that to truly love somebody else in a balanced and healthy way, we have to learn to love ourselves in a balanced and healthy way first.

How do we do that?

By becoming aware, by examining our faulty programming and belief systems. By learning to be ourselves and not the person other people expect us or want us to be.

In recent times I eventually did come up with a definition that now best fits my idea of love.

Love is

Where I can be me
You can be you
And we can be us.

12
"IF I FOLLOW MY RELIGION, BELIEF OR IDEOLOGY WITH GREAT ZEAL, THEN I WILL BE HAPPY."

FALSE
This is almost like an appendix of Act Eleven. The previous Act gave me a really good insight into the origins of my distorted view of love and belonging within the context of the relationships in my family of origin. This Act has shown me how that distortion of thinking played out for me in such a negative way when I left home to go out into the big world.

I believed that I had to fix the world in order to feel love and to be happy. I needed people, and even worse, I felt that people needed me.

However, at the very core my life was meaningless; I was so detached from myself and so unhappy. It eventually brought me to a point where I would have done anything or believed anything just to belong somewhere, to feel valued, to feel like I was a part of something.

I can see now how irrational all of this was. I can see the recklessness of my behavior, my gullibility, how I believed things to be true that I now know were not true.

When we get locked into a way of thinking like I did, and we are pursuing this belief or ideology with such passion, zeal, and fervor, there is no place for discernment. We lose our ability to see the bigger picture.

We cannot see outside of our now very narrow view of the world. Our view of the world has become black or white, my way or no way. Everybody else's point of view becomes a threat, and eventually they become the enemy.

A very important point to remember here:

The more we retreat into this belief and ideology (unknowingly) the further we are going along the continuum into our Red Zone. So, because of our increased anxiety, as we passionately embrace our beliefs, we incrementally (over time) disconnect from our Blue Zone. Now our thinking becomes even more irrational, our view of the world becomes even narrower, and we will feel even more anxious.

The more anxious we become, the further we recede into our Red Zone. Now we are tapping into and reconnecting to all our insecurities, unprocessed feelings of hurt, and unresolved traumas. Meanwhile, messages are being sent to all our cells to say there is an imminent threat, so everything is being mobilized for "fight or flight". This is absolutely guaranteed to make us sick—have no doubt about it—as our whole system is out of balance.

Eventually we end up so far down the continuum away from our Blue Zone, and our thinking becomes so irrational that it now borders on paranoia, and anybody that we perceive does not agree with our viewpoint will become a threat and eventually our enemy. As we are now totally living in our Red Zone, there is absolutely no place for discernment or examination.

If we continue to live in the Red Zone over an extended period of time we will become very unwell, either mentally or physically or both. That is a fact. This is the science of how the human condition functions.

Eventually we get to a point where the belief or ideology that we started out with (and I am not saying that there is a problem with having a belief/ideology, as long as you have awareness) becomes enmeshed with our reconnection to our past hurts, injustices, and angers (and we are not even aware of this). Now these are what are driving us forward.

Because of the increased anxieties and fears that the world now lives in, it would be reasonable to say that society (in the main) is constantly living in the Red Zone. This is becoming more obvious almost on a daily basis. If we remember from earlier reading, constant anxiety leads to a disconnection and a rapid feeling of not belonging within ourselves. We need to feel we belong, so more and more we are connecting to online groups to find this belonging. These groups are becoming more and more polarized in their views. To name but a few:

White Supremacist Groups
Gender-based Groups
Racially-based groups
Groups to the extreme left
Groups to the extreme right

We are fighting all these pseudo wars, on all of these fronts now, and if we are not able to learn discernment, the increased levels of fear and anxiety (as we constantly live in the Red Zone) will destroy the very ecosystem of our humanity. This is incontrovertibly true.

13
"IF I SACRIFICE EVERYTHING FOR OTHERS, INCLUDING MY CAREER, ALL MY POSSESSIONS AND ASPIRATIONS, I WILL BE HAPPY."

FALSE

A number of years ago, I came across a really interesting character who had tracked me down. He told me that he was interested in what I had to say about the world, and wanted to meet up for a chat.

After a number of failed attempts, we finally succeeded in meeting up for a cup of coffee. He was roughly the same age as myself, well-travelled, and had heard about me from a relative of his who had heard me speaking at some event a number of years past.

In a nutshell he had been an extremely successful CEO of a very large company, and had given up everything to live in a Buddhist retreat somewhere in Nepal (not quite *The Monk Who Sold His Ferrari*, but there were similarities).

He spoke of the humble, but very dysfunctional family that he grew up in, of leaving home at sixteen and going to work on a fishing boat, of how he made his first million by the time he was twenty-three years of age, and of how he was a multimillionaire many times over by the time he was thirty.

He spoke of how he was constantly driven by an unrelenting

passion to "escape the unhappy claws of his childhood" and also to show the world "that he was somebody", and how eventually he was hoping to "find happiness".

By the time he was forty-five, he had two failed marriages and was estranged from his family. He woke up one morning and it dawned on him that he was a paradox: "He had never had so much, but at the same time he never had so little".

He made the momentous decision to get rid of everything. He sold everything, and between his children and various charitable organizations, he gave away everything he possessed, upped sticks and went to Nepal, with a view to finding "peace, contentment and happiness".

He spent five years in Nepal, and on the morning, we spoke he was a year out of the monastery, trying to recreate relationships with his estranged family.

After spending all of the time listening to Tom (not real name), I just asked one question:

Did you find what you were looking for?

"No."

What were you looking for?

"Happiness, belonging, peace and contentment."

We met on a number of occasions after that, and Tom eventually moved away.

It was only when I was reading and trying to understand this Act that Tom's story sprang to mind, and his story helped me to clarify what this Act tells us.

Tom's life was entirely about him. From his driven passion and desire to "escape the unhappy claws of his childhood", believing that "he" had to "show the world" and "prove to everybody" that "he" was "somebody", to the giving up of everything and going to live in total isolation in order to "find happiness".

The irony is that none of these things brought him happiness.

Why?

Because it was all about Tom, and as we have discussed in many of the Acts, the world is not "about me"; if it is, we will never be happy. A lot of us have this faulty belief system that says to us, "If we achieve and accumulate and gather lots of attachments, we will be happy", but we won't.

The reality is (and it was most definitely for Tom) we have to make the journey backwards and address the original "wound/trauma" that created our faulty programming in the first place.

Only then can we be truly happy.

14

A. What does not kill you makes you weaker.
B. You are your feelings.
C. The world is made up of either good or bad people.

FALSE

Having worked my way through these Acts a goodly number of times, it is very obvious to me that these three statements are indeed false, and yet you would be astounded by the vast number of people who believe them to be true.

This I am sure in many ways is due to the programmed messages that society has been driving forward with for over two hundred years now, and they are:

"Only the strongest will survive",

"Bigger, Faster, Stronger", and

"You are what you feel".

A. WHAT DOES NOT KILL YOU MAKES YOU WEAKER.

We live in a world now that does not allow us to mess up or to make a mistake. If we make a mistake or mess up now, we will be both judged and executed by the current moral arbitrators of society, the mass media. We will be judged without context. We will be found guilty without a defense. We will then be immediately cancelled for the rest of our lives to the sin bin, with no recourse. We all know this to be true as we all have sat back in recent times and watched the public humiliation of many high-profile figures, as well as many not so high-profile figures.

This gives great substance to the falseness of the above-mentioned statement. The truth, of course, is that the opposite applies.

Some of the greatest positive influencers in politics, industry, sport, and society in general throughout the history of humankind have been people who have made mistakes, made some great errors of judgement, or got it "badly wrong". However, they would have gone away, reflected on their mistakes and difficulties, and come back bigger and stronger as a result; then they were able to pass on this great learning to society at large.

It is only through our mistakes that we learn, and if we are willing to learn from our mistakes, we have the ability to impact on so many people's lives in a positive way.

This wisdom of the ages is lost to a whole generation now because of this falsehood, this idea of creating "a perfect world". We should remind ourselves that it does not exist.

B. YOU ARE YOUR FEELINGS.

We most definitely are not our feelings even though most people would believe that they are. This has been one of the great fallacies of society going right back to when language evolved for the first time.

I spoke earlier on about how I learned through this program to equate feelings and emotions together as a way of understanding. Emotions (e-motions) are just energies being relocated in the body and mind during "fight or flight" responses when we are anxious. Obviously, (and it is designed this way) because of these energies moving in the body, it does not feel good as their purpose is to get you to respond for survival. The purpose of the feeling is to make you aware that something is wrong. So, for this reason feelings are a good thing; they are communicating something to us.

Emotions/feelings have been with us since humankind first existed on the planet. Language is only a recent development in our evolution. It goes to say it has been helpful, but it can also be very unhelpful as we are putting the cart before the horse, and expecting people to put words on what they are feeling. The real reality is there is no language for what we are feeling, it is just a sensation of energy moving in the body, and the more anxious we get, the more disconnected we can become from ourselves and others around us.

There is no question that language is essential: As D. A, Schacter wrote in his 1996 book, Searching for Memory, "Our sense of self depends on being able to organize our memories into a coherent whole". This requires well-functioning connections between The Red Zone and The Blue Zone and the self-system of the body-connections that are often damaged by trauma and anxiety

The starting point of any conversation in a therapeutic setting, or even outside a therapeutic setting, with anybody who is distressed, is to sit them down and just go through some breathing techniques, which immediately bring all the energies back to balance, and settle things down. Within a couple of minutes, we have actually changed the way we are feeling, so from a pure science perspective, we could not be our feelings . At this point we are in a more receptive position to examine the reasons for our anxiety, and learn to understand our faulty programming and belief systems. The full story can only be told after these structures are repaired and after the groundwork had been laid.

This is what you are doing with this program, and I will give you some tips of how I achieved this in Act 5 of The Sixteen Key Actions.

C. THE WORLD IS MADE UP OF GOOD AND BAD PEOPLE.

What these Acts have taught me is the importance of examining things and becoming more aware. As I got better at this, the first question I asked was:

Who decides who is good, and who is bad?

In the modern postindustrial world, the moral arbitrators of society (the mass media who are the new high priests) are deciding who is good and who is bad. This, as I have just spoken about, is having a detrimental effect on society. Within this way of looking at the world, if we make a mistake, we are now "bad" and immediately cancelled, and it is the "good" people who are judging us. It is a "good or bad", "right or wrong", "my way or no way" model, and it leaves no room for examination, compassion, or forgiveness, which are all the benchmarks of a balanced society.

It is not a matter of "good or bad", "right or wrong". It is about understanding that there are consequences for the decisions we make in our lives. It is about learning through our mistakes and coming back with a more examined, lateral view of life.

15
"FEAR, WORRY, ANXIETY, LONELINESS, SORROW, VULNERABILITY, PAIN AND MANY MORE AFFLICTIONS ARE NOT A PART OF SUCCESSFUL LIVING, AND SHOULD BE HIDDEN AND SUPPRESSED".

FALSE
This once again is a myth, a falsehood, and once again just like the last Act probably arrived into society on the back of Darwin's theory of "The Survival of the Fittest" and the idea of "Bigger, Faster, Stronger". The idea being that you could not show any form of weakness, and if you did you would not be successful.

The upshot of that model, of course, is that we learned to suppress all these emotions that we did not understand or did not know what to do with, into our Red Zone.

Although this model has obviously served us well as in the great advances in science, technology and medicine, unfortunately we are now beginning to discover that without the necessary awareness, it is beginning to threaten the very survival of our species.

I think everybody would agree now that we all live in an incredibly fearful and anxious world. This increased societal anxiety means that we are spending a lot of our time in our Red Zone (and we have no awareness of this) which means we are constantly reconnecting to all of these suppressed emotions which can go back generations.

In many ways we have opened the door to our dark side, and the manifestation of these emotions, coupled with the fact that we have no idea what to do with them, is creating a very dark and ugly society which over time, left unchecked, will threaten the very ecosystem of our humanity.

All of these emotions are a normal part of human existence. Under no circumstance should they be suppressed, as ultimately, they will kill us.

Through this program I have become aware that it is not the "strongest" and the "fittest" who will survive.

It is the ones who become aware, and who learn to adapt.

16

"YOUR LIFE IS A SHAMBLES, IN GREAT DISORDER, AND YOU ARE BLINDLY PARTICIPATING IN LIFE, ROBOTICALLY, TO ORDER, WITHOUT EVER THINKING OF WHY YOU DO WHAT YOU DO."

TRUE

Having worked my way through the last thirty-one Acts, I now know what Socrates meant when he said, "The unexamined life is not worth living".

Sometimes we have to lose everything, before we can find anything.

I had to examine all of my faulty beliefs, my programming, a lifetime of running blindfolded, totally unaware, lonely, constantly crying in the dark, feeling miserable, before I could finally accept the above Act.

Once we arrive at that location, and we accept that in many ways we were powerless over most of what happened, our life will never be the same again.

We are now in a position to start the next part of the journey, but only this time we will have a map, a compass, and a wonderful companion called awareness, which of course means we are now journeying without the blindfold.

When that blindfold comes off for the first time, the world can seem a very scary place, but the difference now is that we know we are going to be okay. All we have to do is put one foot in front of the other and stay going.

I used the first two sets of Acts (the "Sixteen Axioms" and the "Sixteen False Beliefs") almost like a mantra. I did not have to fully understand them or fully act on them; I just repeated them over and over in my head. I also learned to allow my body to fully experience them. I could feel a lovely sense of "knowing" developing within me, and for the first time I felt that I was going to be ok.

One might ask, how did I know? The answer!! I didn't know. But through this program, here is what I learned: I wrote in chapter two about the science of how the brain and mind evolved.

Our biological and emotional brain evolved first, over many millions of years. Because our rational, conscious, analytical brain did not evolve for millions of years our earlier ancestors did not have the ability to, analyse, to make decisions based on cognitive rational or creating choices. This meant that we evolved glacially, very slowly, over a long period of time. But we did survive and evolve. How was this so? Because we had an emotional and biological brain that was linked to our gut. This was how we developed instinct, gut instinct, trust, our body knew. It knew through our five senses, so when danger was present, whatever that danger was, our five senses of sound, sight, touch, taste and smell would inform us that everything was not ok, and would not be okay if we did not respond. So, we learned how to respond, in order to survive, and that is how we evolved. It is only when the rational brain evolved that our evolution started to speed up, and allowed the advancement of society as we know it today, with all our discoveries, innovations of science, medicine and technology. But sadly, it has come at a cost, as we have disconnected from that part of us that was the cornerstone of our evolution, trust, belonging, gut instinct.

I have learned with the benefit of this programme how to reconnect to my body. I learned a mantra; "Get out of my head and into my body". How did I do that? Through breathing. The more I practiced stopping for a couple of minutes a number of times a day, just to breathe, focus on the oxygen going through my body, and by doing this, shutting down the thoughts in my head. By continually and persistently doing this, over time, I reconnected to my original biological and emotional brain. All of a sudden, I began to develop trust, a sense of belonging to myself (for the first time ever) and an instinctual gut knowing that everything was going to be ok. I just knew. I knew because I had reconnected to something that has been there for millions of years. I became well, I know that you can also. All I had to do now was act, and that is what the next Sixteen Key Actions are all about.

THE LAYMAN'S GUIDE TO THE "SIXTEEN KEY ACTIONS"

I

"YOU HAVE COME TO THE REALIZATION THAT ALL IS NOT WELL IN YOUR LIFE. THOUGH THIS MAY BE ADDICTION, DEPRESSION, ANXIETY, CONTROLLING OR TOXIC RELATIONSHIPS, FEARS NAMED OR UNNAMED, TRAUMA AND RESENTFUL DISSATISFACTION, YOU ARE UNHAPPY AND YOUR LIFE IS OUT OF CONTROL".

Having worked my way through the "Sixteen Axioms" and the "Sixteen False Beliefs", I came to the realization that I had spent most of my life marinating in the molten lava from the trauma of my early life and its subsequent faulty programming.

And just to recap: the sexual abuse was the original event/events, and the molten lava was the burning feelings that I constantly ran away from, as I could not understand them or cope with them on a daily basis, such as:

Fear
Hopelessness
Constant sense of unease and dread
Shame
Hurt
Guilt
Anger, etc.

My inability to cope with all of this had subsequently led me down a pathway of unhelpful coping mechanisms and patterns of maladaptive behaviors which led to great difficulties in my life, and in the lives of others close to me.

For me, these 48 Acts were the ultimate dawning of awareness.

This was the first time in nearly all of my life that something deep down inside me was telling me that I was going to be okay. It was not that anything had significantly changed in my life; the problems were still there, I still felt awful, but something deep within me just seemed to know.

I had acquired enough knowledge and understanding in the first two sets of Acts to allow me to feel a quiet confidence building within. I knew that there was not going to be a quick fix or a quick rush to wellness. I did not have to just accept that these things happened in my life and then somehow magically get on with the rest of my life.

I did not have to accept anything at this moment as acceptance takes time. For me it was a realization that:

"All is not well in my life".

My life had become unmanageable, but because I did not have awareness, I was powerless to do anything about the things that had happened on my life's journey up to now.

With the awareness I was now coming into I realized that there was something I could do to change. I did not know how just yet, but I was open to learning and making a commitment to myself to do the best that I could, and work from the inside out to make the necessary changes.

I also knew that I was not alone and that I did not have to do it all on my own. It was up to me to reach out and let people who cared into my very fractured world. I knew from following this program that I now had a template, which was based on truth and reality, to help and to guide me on the journey that I was about to embark on.

At this moment it was all about learning how to sit in the feelings, but not to run away from them or marinate in them anymore.

2

"YOU ADMIT THAT YOU DO NOT UNDERSTAND THE REASON WHY YOUR LIFE IS LIKE THIS, OR IF YOU DO, THAT TO WHICH YOU ATTRIBUTE THE REASON WHY, IS PROBABLY INCORRECT."

As I pointed out at the end of the last Act, for me, it was about learning to sit in the feelings that I was experiencing but not to marinate in them, and in particular not to react to them, which is what I would have spent most of my life doing. This was exceptionally difficult for me, as it was beginning to dawn on me that most of what I perceived to be true was not actually true, and it almost felt as if my whole life had been one big lie.

I came to the realization of two things.

A. I didn't understand the reasons why I felt the way I felt.

B. I was mistaken about the things that caused me to behave and do the things I did, because I misattributed the reasons. In other words, in effect my problems could never be solved because I had a double whammy—I did not understand, and when I thought I understood, I was wrong.

To the observer that may be the way it looked, but for me, the way I learned to survive in the world was my absolute reality, and it was the only way that I knew. As I was now becoming aware for the first time, I was also feeling very vulnerable and scared, and I really had to work hard to learn to be gentle with myself and not beat myself up over things that I did wrong or that I should have seen and known better.

The reality is that I didn't know. I had no awareness, so how could I have done things any differently?

The difference now is that through the dawning of awareness, I do know, and I now have a responsibility to begin the journey of change.

For me, one of the really difficult things in this Act was to start to trust and let people into my very fractured and scared world. Ideally, we would like to have someone to talk to who can listen to us and understand us when we are feeling emotional and confused, especially at a time like this when we are feeling particularly vulnerable and fragile.

For any of us who have lived lives of fear and high anxiety, trust can be a difficult concept to achieve, in particular when you are not quite sure who you can trust in the first place. We would have spent a lot of our lives pushing people away and isolating ourselves, and the thought that we are suddenly going to open up and talk about what we are feeling almost borders on delusional.

However, I would say that my experience of this Act would compel me to point out that if you are somebody who is delving into your past story and history for the first time, it would be very beneficial to seek out a therapist (and make sure you ask around for guidance in selecting a therapist) to assist you on the early stages of your journey. The early part of the journey can be very overwhelming, and a therapist can hold you in a safe place and assist you to work through these difficult first steps.

Also, for somebody like me who carried a lot of stored traumas, a medical intervention was very beneficial to dampen down those Red Zone receptors which were switched on 24/7 and needed medication in the short term to help switch them off. That subsequently helped me to engage in the therapeutic process with a clearer head.

None of this is to say that we should not feel these emotions that we might now be experiencing. However, it is not helpful to try to analyze what we are feeling at this moment. Remember we cannot rationalize an emotion; I should know as I have spent an entire life trying to do this and coming up with false narratives to try to achieve this. In the meantime, all I was doing was suppressing the emotions and convincing myself that I was right and everybody else was wrong.

Always remember that emotions are just energies moving in the body, and although they may feel uncomfortable, they cannot do us any harm. The maladaptive behaviors that we used to escape from these feelings are what caused the difficulties in our life in the first place, not the feelings themselves.

Simply learn to take a moment to feel the hurt or sadness or anger. Over time, if we allow yourself to sit with it, learn to trust it, and let it run its course, we will be okay no matter what is going on around us. Always remember the darkest nights we have experienced are just like storms: they always pass, and the sun always comes back out eventually. So, just learn to trust what we are feeling, and allow it to happen naturally and over time.

This is just the beginning. Every one of us, through our faulty programming and false beliefs, learned a role to survive in childhood. The most important thing that I learned in this Act is that we are not stuck with these roles and programming, and that over time we can change them.

That is what truly changed my life.

ॐ 3 ॐ
"YOU REALIZE THAT YOU ARE LIVING AN INAUTHENTIC FALSE LIFE, AND THAT YOU ARE UNAWARE AND LACK THE ABILITY TO LIVE IN THE WORLD."

When people read these Acts, they will read them for very different reasons. For some it will be out of curiosity; others will probably approach it as another book in the hundreds of self-help publications they would have read as they searched for the reasons for their own unhappiness.

For me it was because I had arrived at an impasse in my life, and I was in a deep crisis. When you arrive in crisis you generally end up with two choices: the first one is denial (you can become angry and righteous and look to blame everybody else for your present circumstances), and the second one is honestly asking yourself (as I learned from these Acts), "How has my programming brought me to this moment?"

I can tell you, with my hand on my heart, that with the help of this program, and by the time I got to this particular Act, I was determined for the first time to begin the most painful but ultimately the most rewarding journey I have ever taken in my entire life: THE JOURNEY OF DISCOVERING MY OWN TRUTH.

The first question I asked myself was,

What is the truth?

Now there is the six-million-dollar question. What is the truth?

The answer? Mmmmm!!

This is a very complex question. In many ways it can depend on the context. Here are a few examples.

The truth is whatever you want it to be.

The truth is whatever the other person wants it to be.

The truth is whatever the group or organization wants it to be.

Looking back on my life I can now see that it is almost like there were two of me. There was the me that I wanted the world to see and know, and then there was the me that I did not want the world to see and know. And it gets even more complex as I did not even know the me that I kept private from the world.

I just wanted the world to see this popular, happy, well-educated person who was always on top of things, but that was not my reality. That was the inauthentic me, and subsequently I was not being true to myself. It is not that I intentionally went around telling lies, I was really just covering up the part of myself that I did not understand or could not cope with, often out of fear of judgement, recrimination and shame.

When we live an inauthentic and false life, we live a life of fear, pretending everything is okay when it is not okay. It is a life of perception and optics; we want everybody to see us as somebody that, deep down, we know we are not.

With the help of this Act, I can now see that truth is existence. Truth is reality.

When we learn to be truthful and honest with ourselves (and that is a difficult thing to achieve) fear dissipates. When we live in truth, there is no fear.

When we live in truth, we live in reality, and when we live in reality, we just know that no matter how difficult things may get in our life in the future, we will be okay.

How do I know? Because I am okay today, and if I am okay today, I just know that I will be okay in time to come. I do not live in fear anymore. I am not at home all day or in my bed at night not able to sleep because I am worrying about something I think might be going to happen in the future, or something that people might find out about me.

I do not spend my days anymore worrying about things that have not happened, because that is not reality. The reality for me now is that I accept that things will happen in the future, but I certainly cannot do anything about them today. That will only keep me locked into the anxiety response, which I now know is going to make me sick.

But I do know, that when things happen in the future, which is inevitable, I will be okay and I will deal with them when and if it happens. You cannot deal with something today that you think might happen next week, or next month, or next year. The something you think might be going to happen is what is keeping you sick today, as the constant worry is keeping you stuck in the Red Zone, fighting off invisible threats.

I did not avoid living in truth and reality because I was this bad person; no, I avoided my reality because it was too painful, and the truth of it was that my hidden reality was too painful to face.

You will often hear the phrase the truth hurts, and it does, which is why we often do not live in the truth of our reality. How we really feel can hurt so bad, and we are not able to cope with the intensity of the feelings.

Part of the great learning I have been experiencing with this program is that yes, the truth does hurt, but only in the short term. After the initial hurt and pain is understood, owned and experienced, the world of truth and reality will be one of the most rewarding experiences we will ever have.

❈ 4 ❦
"YOU RESOLVE TO EMPOWER YOURSELF THROUGH SELF-KNOWLEDGE."

Never in the history of our world have we had so much knowledge, information, data, etc., all instantly accessible at the press of a button. Within an instant we can have information on almost any topic that we could care to mention or think about.

There are multibillion-dollar industries thriving on data and information. I think it is fair to say that by far the most valuable commodity that now exists in the world, is data.

The consumer, materialistic, capitalistic model of industry has crossed all thresholds of society now. Take education as an example. We pride ourselves now as the most educated generation of all generations. The literacy rates around the world have never been so good. Look at the huge numbers that go to college now. The world has never had so many so called "educated experts". Education is a massive industry; look at all the grind schools, the grind teachers. They tell us that now, a masters degree is the "new degree" and that the PhD is the "new masters". Of course, this is all good, but we must have balance.

I bought into all of this, as I believed that with all of my knowledge and education I would be somebody that people would look up to. It was all about the titles, the letters you could have after your name; people would really think I was somebody.

And I really believed I was somebody. People would often tell me that I was "amazing" and that I had a "breadth of knowledge" about almost every subject. People looked up to me; I was on a roller coaster. This was how I identified myself.

Sadly, as I was about to find out, although I had all the knowledge about everything that was to be known about the world outside myself, I had no knowledge about the world inside myself. This was to be my Achilles' heel.

It struck me when I came to this Key Action that there is not one academic principle that teaches us, or prepares us, to know what it is like to be an emotional human being in the world.

We have driven forward for the past two hundred years, molding and creating our educational models around educating the cognitive brain, and at the same time almost completely ignoring that we have a preexisting emotional and biological brain that we have never been educated about. And ironically, as the anxiety levels of the world increase, this is the part of the brain we are primarily working from. We really cannot see the damage this is having on our society.

It is so ironic that we now live in a world where we have never had so much education, we have never had so many experts, and yet the world has never been in such a crisis. Interesting, isn't it?

This is probably pointing us to the fact that our models of education are too narrow and one-dimensional, are widely modelled on educating the cognitive brain, and are completely out of sync with the fearful, competitive world we are trying to survive in.

I discovered in this Act that I had no self-knowledge. I had no sense of belonging and identity. I identified myself by labels. I did not know how to live within me, as no one ever taught me.

I can now see that we (in particular our children and young people) are being taught how to live from all the wrong places, where there is no differentiation between fact and fiction, and where the truth has no meaning. A large number of people in the present information-driven world believes everything they see, hear, and read, and have no sense of discernment or examination.

My grandmother had a great saying; she told us, "We should believe nothing of what we hear, and only half of what we see". Whatever we are hearing, seeing and reading, we need to take the time to examine and evaluate, to allow ourselves to understand context and balance, and to learn to be able to separate fact from fiction.

It is only by creating self-awareness, isolating the truth and sticking to the truth no matter how painful it is, that we can give our lives meaning.

This Act and the previous Act have taught me that without self-awareness, we have no chance of getting well. We have to understand all of our past, all of our environments, all of our anxieties, and learn to create awareness around them. As Winston Churchill once said, "Those who fail to learn from history are doomed to repeat it".

We have to learn to know who we are and what that knowing means. Knowing means relinquishing all the triteness, programming and beliefs that have been engendered in us since the day we were born.

We then start to see who we truly are, and take it from me, when you get to that place you will be pleasantly surprised with who you truly are.

5
"SEEK KNOWLEDGE NO MATTER WHAT THE COST."

Knowledge leads to understanding. Understanding leads to awareness. Awareness leads to wellness.

As pointed out in the previous Act, there is a huge amount of knowledge and information available at the touch of a button now, and it can be very difficult to figure out what is helpful and what is not. In my lifetime of constantly seeking knowledge and information to try to understand why I felt the way I was feeling, I ended up going down many wrong roads and made many mistakes, as I had no way of discerning what was helpful and what was unhelpful.

I have subsequently learned to categorize knowledge and information into two categories: what is nice to know, and what is important to know.

This helped me not to have information overload and also provided balance, which is the key to wellness.

It struck me that my life was like a jigsaw puzzle. Imagine if we purchased a jigsaw puzzle with ten thousand pieces and sat down on the floor to attempt to put it together. What is the one thing we could not start without?

The lid of the box, of course. The lid of the box has the picture, the vision of what we are trying to achieve, and even with the lid of the box it would still be incredibly difficult to put together the ten thousand pieces on our own.

In many ways this is what our lives are like. We are in possession of this wonderful creation called the human organism, with hundreds of millions of very intricate components and parts, and absolutely no idea of how it works or does not work, as nobody ever taught us; we have no picture (no lid of the box).

In this Act I came to the realization that although most of what was going on externally was outside my control, my new found knowledge was leading me to understand that what was going on internally in my own brain, mind and body was actually inside my control. I just had to be willing to make a start on the journey of understanding.

I am thirty-six Acts into this program now, and I have developed a greater broadening of my understanding and awareness of myself. It has given me the confidence to present to you, over the next number of pages, an overview of the increased understanding and awareness which were bringing me closer to wellness.

In a nutshell, I just started to put together a set of repetitive practices (none of which are new) but with a different perspective and understanding, that I found helpful in order to assist me on my journey, and that could be used to switch off the automatic flow of anxiety that I constantly experienced and to help bring the mind and the body back into balance, into the moment, and into wellbeing.

It works by telling our mind, brain and body what to do through repetitive practices of reality (rather than perceptions), breathing, sharing, writing and self-talking, as well as monitoring the inputs of information that we put into your body, brain and mind.

Ready to go? Good!!

I began to figure out over time that there were similarities between how the human organism (namely ourselves) operated, and how computers operated.

Let us say that we buy a 10,000-euro computer and put it on our kitchen table, still in its box. Even before we take it out of the box, there is a certain amount of information put on the hard drive during production that we had no say over; it was there when we bought it.

Wouldn't that be fair to say?

Well, in the same way we humans are the same. There was a certain amount of information entered on our hard drive during production in the womb, like instinct and nature, that we had no say over. It was present on our hard drive when we came out of the womb.

Do we agree with that? Good!!

Let us now take the computer out of the box, leave it on the table, and look at it for a number of minutes. It will not do anything, will it? No, it needs energy; we have to power it up from an energy source.

We were the same. When we arrived out of the womb, we needed a source of energy, namely oxygen. We took our first breath and through a process of respiration, oxygen is metabolized into energy, and life is born.

It works the same for both the computer and people; if there is not enough energy, there will be problems. If there is too much energy, there will also be problems. It must be balanced.

With me so far? Good!!

Okay, let us plug in our computer, switch it on and get ready to go.

We will sit and watch the computer for the next twenty minutes. It will not do anything, will it?

What is it waiting for?

You've got it, an input of information.

So let us start typing and keying information into the computer. Now even though the computer is worth 10,000 euro, wouldn't it be fair to say that the computer has no way of knowing whether we are giving it the right information or the wrong information?

It just trusts us and puts the information on the hard drive without question or judgement.

Well, guess what? Our brain, mind and body are the same, they just work on inputs of information. They do not question or make judgment, they stick it on the hard drive.

Through these 48 Acts, I figured out that in order for me to be well, and to try to live a life of balanced peace and contentment, I had to start monitoring and understanding these inputs of information, and begin the journey of rewriting my own programming.

We input information into the human organism in a number of ways.

BREATHING
NATURE AND INSTINCT
(happens in the womb before birth)
PROGRAMMING
(the messages we receive from parents, family, guardians, teachers and society in general, which are very powerful in the first seven years of life; also, the roles and personas we take on from early life)
THOUGHTS
(the messages that I give my mind and body through my thinking)
DIET
(my mind, brain, and body respond in different ways to the food I eat, the liquid I drink, and the substances I put in)
EXERCISE (OR LACK OF)
ENVIRONMENTAL FACTORS

Our breathing is definitely the most important place to start with, as a proper understanding of breath can help to ground us in a safe place when we find ourselves dealing with difficult thoughts or experiences on our journey towards understanding and awareness.

Now, just a quick recap on what I have written previously.

When in high anxiety, the body and brain are locked into a "fight, flight or freeze" response and our sympathetic nervous system is busy pumping energy through the system. This is like somebody having their foot on the car accelerator, pumping petrol continuously throughout the system.

While this is happening your breathing becomes compromised and shallow, as energies (oxygen, blood, chemicals) are being diverted away from the visceral block to the reflex block. If you remain in this state of arousal over a sustained period of time, it can have calamitous implications for the entire human organism.

The second branch of the autonomic system is the parasympathetic nervous system (PNS) which is the opposite of the SNS.

If the SNS is the petrol pump with its foot on the accelerator, the PNS is the brake which slows it all down, promoting self-protective functions like digestion and wound healing. It triggers the release of acetylcholine to put a break on arousal, slowing the heart down, relaxing muscles, and returning breathing to normal, thus bringing the entire human organism back to a normal state of balance (homeostasis).

I hope you are beginning to see that how we breathe has a massive say in how the human condition functions.

Most of us would not even be aware that our breathing was being compromised constantly by our anxiety.

The reason for this, of course, is that most of us would not recognize that we were anxious in the first place. A lot of people's anxiety can be very passive and not instantly recognizable. Most of us see the anxious person as the one who is on edge or worrying all the time, but anxiety can often be hidden from the public view by our programming and the roles and personas we learned in childhood. So, we can be a little bit like the swan, with the graceful, serene part that we see gliding on top of the water, and do not see the part that is flapping like mad under the water.

So, seeing as breathing gives life, and if we stop breathing, we die, it makes great sense to have a deeper awareness about our breathing. Awareness of breath keeps you in the moment, and when we learn to trust it, we also learn to trust the moment. With practice that moment can become a safe place for us, no matter what we are thinking or feeling elsewhere.

We are breathing automatically all the time, which means that most of us do not think about how we are breathing or what kind of benefits we can get from it.

As you are sitting there reading this, take a deep breath in, and as you inhale, observe whether your tummy is going in or out!!

It should be going out; however, do not be surprised to feel that your tummy is going in as you inhale.

It should be going out on the inhale, but as most of us are now living in the Red Zone as a result of our fear-driven society, our breathing is shallow a lot of the time, and we do not even realize that our breathing is going inwards.

Good, balanced breathing is essential for wellness, more so now than ever before, as we live in a world of exponential fear, competitiveness and conflict.

It is a habit that we have to create.

Getting into this habit takes some practice, as it takes some time to become mindful and aware.

Like many things, it is just a matter of keeping it simple. It starts with just creating a little bit more awareness around our breathing, and the fact that our body is breathing, by pausing at different times throughout the day to take notice.

So, as you are sitting there reading this, I want you to close your eyes for a moment and become aware that your body is gently breathing all the time.

Experience the gentle rise and fall of your tummy.

If any thoughts enter your head, or there is any conflict with what is going on in your head and what is going on in your body, just observe it, let it pass, and then go back to noticing your breathing.

Just sit there quietly with your breathing.

Acknowledge the breath at the point of entry, feeling the cool dry air that comes in at the tip of the nose and then down into the tummy.

Feel the tummy rising up and expanding, hold this for the count of five.

Slowly exhale out through the mouth on the count of five, and notice that a warm moist air leaves the body.

Do these four or five times. Inhaling on the count of five, holding, then exhaling on the count of five.

When you open your eyes, you should notice that your body and mind have relaxed.

This is because you have turned off your SNS (petrol pump) and turned on your PNS (brake), which means a healing energy is now moving through your body. Acetylcholine has been released, which relaxes the body.

Also, while doing this breathing practice you are learning to reconnect to your emotional and biological brain, which is the part of you that knows you are going to be ok, and over time you will become aware of trust and belonging beginning to develop.

Think of the benefit this could have for you if you brought it into your life more often every day. As I said earlier, this takes a lot of practice, so having a few good prompts to remind you would be a good idea.

I wear a blue band on my wrist, and I have little blue dots placed in different places around my home, my workplace, my car, etc.

The idea is that every time I have a visual of my blue band or blue dots, I pause to take a meaningful breath. I find that this works really well for me, as that mindful breath brings me back to the Blue Zone when my racing or disturbed thoughts have brought me into the Red Zone.

Over time, deeper, more mindful breathing will become more of a reflex for you, both in everyday moments, and in high pressure situations, helping you to respond rationally from the Blue Zone rather than react irrationally from the Red Zone.

All the time, while consistently practicing this, you are creating awareness, which in turn promotes wellness.

In my own lifelong journey of trying to understand my struggles with fear and anxiety and their negative impact on my wellbeing, I came across hundreds, if not thousands, of studies and pieces of research that helped me to have a greater understanding of why living in a prolonged state of anxiety and fear are having such a negative impact on the health and wellbeing of society in the present moment.

Three particular studies were of great value to me, and I will briefly mention them here, as they are important. They are important because they point out the absolute truth and reality of what I am talking about. Breathing and breath are not just some nice things you do at a spa day, or on a wellness day; they are vital to our very survival.

To understand these concepts is absolutely vital to the very survival of our species, as we now consistently live far too much of our lives in our Red Zone.

The greatest casualty of constantly living in the Red Zone is the constant disruption to flow and supply of blood and oxygen as respiration changes.

Bruce Lipton, PhD in his terrific book *The Biology of Belief*, and indeed in his many workshops and presentations which I have attended on many occasions, has a great way of describing why constantly living in the Red Zone is making us sicker and sicker.

This is how I interpreted his great message, and it was to be of great benefit to me on my journey to recovery:

"When the receptor picks up the threat in the external environment, it immediately informs the effector for the fight, flight or freeze response. The effector informs the cells to prepare them for danger. Remember, all we are is trillions of cells covered in cling film, and every cell has a liver, a kidney, a heart, a brain, a memory, etc. It is the cell that informs the genes. When this keeps happening on a regular basis, our whole internal environment changes and becomes unhealthy, which is why we get sick; we get sick in unhealthy environments".

We get sick in unhealthy environments. When we live our lives in the Red Zone, our breathing is compromised on a constant basis, which can create a very unhealthy internal environment. This can have massive consequences on our wellbeing.

Two other scientists really came to my attention during my obsessive trawling of research and literature. And remember my obsession with trying to understand why we get sick had nothing to do with wanting to be an expert on all things medical. This was all about my survival. As I mentioned earlier, when I discovered the Adverse Childhood Experience study, my score on their matrix showed that because of my own adverse childhood experiences, I had a much higher chance of contracting a life-threatening illness in my adult years. I needed to know why.

Also, the challenge of this Act is to "seek self-knowledge no matter what the cost".

The two scientists whose work I found fascinating and very relevant to me in particular were Dr. Otto Warburg and Walter Fiers.

Dr. Warburg was awarded a Nobel Prize in 1931 for discovering that low oxygen was the primary characteristic of all cancer cells. He discovered that cancer cells were low in oxygen due to a change in cellular respiration, from using oxygen for respiration to using fermentation of sugar, which is an ancient form of energy metabolism.

In the words of Dr. Warburg:

"Cancer above all other diseases has countless secondary causes, including environmental. But, even for cancer, there is only one prime cause. Summarized in a few words, the prime cause of cancer is the replacement of the respiration of oxygen in normal body cells by a fermentation of sugar".

The second scientist that jumped out at me was Walter Fiers, a Belgian molecular biologist. Fiers, along with a team of researchers in the 1970s discovered the Tumor Necrosis Factor (TNF). Necrosis is a decay or death of cells because of blood flow problems, deoxygenation, diseases or injury. The study looked at how dead cells came together to form a mass which formed the tumor. Now I will admit the study was very complicated, but very significant, particularly in the treatment of cancer. But the one piece that Fiers said that really stuck out for me was,

"In all our study and research we never once saw a TNF in a human body that had homeostasis."

I now know for the first time that we do not just get sick. We get sick for a reason, and that reason is the unease (anxiety) that is created when we live our life in the Red Zone, the constant "fight, flight, freeze" mode of modern life that our human organism is not designed to live in.

The more anxious we become, the more deoxygenated our cells become, and the more we experience blood flow problems.

We are making ourselves sick and we do not realize it, because we do not have awareness. It is like putting a bucket under a dripping tap; the tap is dripping away all the time into the bucket. At some point it will only take one drop to overflow the bucket. Then we spend all our time trying to analyze the final drop, which we believe overflowed the bucket. But it was not the final drop; it was all the drops beforehand that we were never aware of, and subsequently never took time to empty the bucket.

We are the same, because of the fearful, highly anxious environments that we are now trying to survive in. Through our lack of awareness, we do not realize that the bucket is filling up, and at some point it will spill over and we will get sick.

We have got to become aware and start to empty that bucket at regular intervals.

The one thing that is absolutely guaranteed to balance that bucket is awareness of breath.

Our breathing is our greatest ally and friend. It is free, it is under our nose, it is instantly accessible, and it can save our lives.

I am not saying that our breathing will cure us if we are already sick, but it will help our recovery. If you are sick in mind or body, please attend your primary physician or health expert. Your symptoms will have to be treated.

What I am talking about here is the absolute power of awareness of breath in preventing you from getting sick in the first place.

Learning and applying all of this knowledge about breathing was a game changer for me, and it could be for you also.

It is life-giving, lifesaving, and life-changing; practice it and nurture it.

EXERCISE

The next step, now that I had my blood and oxygen flowing better with my breathing, was to take the next level through exercise. I had been a swimmer since childhood, and my military days involved a lot of fitness, but it was only in recent times as I came into recovery that I really made the connection between exercise and wellbeing.

If our cells are suffering from being deprived of oxygen, and at the same time living in the Red Zone is keeping our anxiety levels high by pumping out adrenaline and overloading our bodies with excess energy, then exercise has to be part of the solution, because it burns excess energy. For people with low energy, exercise also has the benefit of getting that energy moving.

We are born to move; we need to move. By not moving, we create inertia and build up negative energy.

I exercise every day, as that is what works for me. When I talk about exercising every day, I mean 35-40 minutes of a good walk, a good swim, a good run, whatever you fancy. I do not mean distance running or endurance training; obviously, most of us cannot do that every day. I'm talking about moving every day for 35-40 minutes, consistently and persistently: walking, jogging, swimming, riding a bike, playing football or tennis, just getting moving.

As with breathing practice, this means creating a good habit by creating balance between the Red Zone and the Blue Zone, and putting your mind and body back into balance. Exercise will become a normal behavior for you, and your body will love you for it. Wellness is about balance.

DIET

All of these inputs like breathing and exercise help us to focus on how to regulate and balance the energy that is in our body and brain, but the Red Zone is also triggered by the energy we put into our system through what we eat and drink.

What you eat and drink has a huge effect on how your brain and body work. Your brain requires more energy than any other organ in your body, and what you eat and drink can either calm you down or make you feel nervous.

I want to make it very clear here that I am not referring to a weight loss plan, and certainly not a quick fix one. Our grandmothers probably had it right where diet is concerned:

"A little bit of what you fancy, and everything in moderation".

As to what you should eat, a lot of research and commentary out there will advise us what foods will have certain benefits for our mind and body. All I can discuss is what works for me (which may not necessarily work for you). I try to eat natural foods rather than processed foods, I try to choose seasonal and plant-based foods wherever I can, and I try to have as much variety and balance as possible. If you have food intolerance difficulties, make sure you seek advice from a dietician or a nutritionist before you embark on any eating plan.

Equally important is what not to eat. From a diet and food perspective, two of the biggest culprits (for me) were sugar and caffeine. Sugar does give your brain energy in the form of glucose, which boosts your thought processing and in moderate doses helps to stabilize your moods, but most of us get too much of a good thing and put our bodies out of balance.

Having too much simple sugar in our bloodstream can destabilize our mood, cause tension and anxiety, and keep us stuck in the Red Zone.

Caffeine has the exact same effect. If we are already overly anxious and living in our Red Zone, the last thing we need is a stimulant in the form of caffeine.

I am not saying we have to give up all of these things, but we do need to create awareness around them.

Hydrate Hydrate Hydrate

I cannot overemphasize the importance of hydration. We have been given this beautiful human organism that needs water to grow. I drink between six and eight glasses of water every day without fail. Your mind, brain and body will love you for it.

When we embark on a healthier regime of awareness around diet, exercise and breathing, one of the most important things is to be gentle with ourselves. Rome was not built in a day, so give yourself time to change and keep persisting with it.

Too many of us have become destination-focused, rather than being mindful of the journey. My solution to this is just to focus on short-term goals:

What do I need to do today?

What do I need to do this week?

What do I need to do when this week is over?

This means having a plan for each day and each week, a sense of purpose, and a sense of vision, in general terms what each day will involve.

Every day should have a time to eat. A time to play. It should have a time to work, a time to rest. It should have a time to pray, or meditation or any other form of taking some time to be alone and quiet. Every day should have a time for exercise, a time for mindful breathing and a time for meaningful communication with other human beings; if it's our nearest and dearest, all the better. Remember it is all about balance.

It is so important for every day to have different components in order to interrupt the automatic flow of Red Zone living. Our brain will keep us going back to the same place forever if we let it, so we have to tell it what to do at every opportunity, and even if we reach a different destination than the one, we had planned, it does not necessarily matter. What really matters is that we are safe on the journey and that we are enjoying it.

MANAGE YOUR THINKING

The trick after making the plan is to get out and do it. Writing down things can help us get where we want to go. In this case, we can take some time to write down the things that we are overthinking and worrying about. Then cross off the things that we cannot do anything about—because we cannot do anything about them. If we have something left that we can do something about, then we can go and do it.

That is the problem for a lot of us (it was for me anyway). We think about doing it, but we don't do it; instead, we procrastinate. But by not acting, we create a fear around it, and then we are back in the Red Zone. Procrastinating keeps us living in our survival brain, which keeps us tapping into our sense of inadequacies from the faulty belief systems that we learned in childhood, which make us feel even more inadequate in the present.

So, make the list, cross out what you cannot do, find out what you can do—and then go do it. There are some of us who "think" all of the time and never actually "do" anything, and then there are others who "do" all of the time and never stop to "think".

It is all about balance.

REWRITING THE PROGRAMME

To be able to live effectively in the balance of the continuum of the Blue Zone and Red Zone, it is vital to be able to understand the faulty programming of our belief systems and roles that we learned in childhood. Our Red Zone will keep a faulty belief system going forever unless we reprogram it.

To break our cycle, our brain must be told what to do. For example, I write with my right hand; all those years ago, for whatever reason, that is the hand I first took the pen in. Did I know how to write? No! I actually had to tell my brain what to do, and through the teaching of my teacher, practice and repetition, time and effort, I learned how to write with my right hand.

I write really well with my right hand, but I would not be able to write with my left hand. Why? Because I never told my brain I wanted to use my left hand. The only message it ever got was from my right hand.

But if I was unfortunate enough to lose my right hand in the morning, would I learn to use my left hand? You bet I would. By persistently and consistently using my left hand, eventually I would be writing just fine with it. Our brain will do whatever we tell it to do if we tell it often enough, and if we are willing to work hard and take personal responsibility and stop blaming other people because we cannot use our right hand anymore.

If we want to change, we really can.

So, if I am telling myself that I am an idiot and that I am never going to be good enough, then that is the way I am going to be, because my brain does what I tell it. But if I tell myself that I am good enough, then over time my brain will start to believe that instead.

This is where I found writing practices very helpful in bringing me back from Red Zone thinking to Blue Zone thinking.

It separates the different thoughts and emotions and helps us figure out where they are really coming from. Firstly, when thoughts and emotions are stirring in our brain, the art of writing takes us back to the Blue Zone as writing is a front brain activity. So, as we are writing down our thoughts, we have interrupted the automatic flow of Red Zone thinking, a very powerful thing to do.

Secondly, by writing it down, we have a hard copy of what is going on in our head—which is also a very powerful step, because now we are in charge, which means we can challenge these thoughts and begin to rewrite our programming. Also, when we write to ourselves we do not have to worry about other people's judgement – we just listen to our own thoughts and be able to challenge them and rewrite them in the safety of our own time and space.

We can change it from "I feel useless all the time" to "I don't want to feel useless anymore, so I am going to learn to be myself and focus on the many ways that I am useful, both to myself and others." It is our program, and we can turn it around however we like.

Let's look at an example of you as you are walking along the street. You see a friend walking towards you, but he or she crosses to the other side without saying hello. Would your first thought be positive or negative? If you have awareness and you have worked on personal development, you might be able to say to yourself calmly, "Either he did not say hello because he did not see me, or he did see me and decided to say nothing, but that is not my fault. I will give him a call later; he might have something on his mind".

Believe you me, that would be a very rare initial response. If you read about the science of how our brain works in an earlier chapter, you will recall that if there is any sort of perception of a threat in our immediate environment, the message goes immediately to our Red Zone to be processed before it arrives in the Blue Zone.

This means that our first initial thought is more often than not a negative: What did I do wrong? This immediately takes you deeper into the Red Zone (namely your hippocampus) that relates new input to past experiences. Now you remember all the people in your life who ignored you or did not say hello, which makes your next response even more irrational: "He really must not like me".

Now the message is sent to the hypothalamus and the brain stem, recruiting the stress hormone system and the autonomic nervous system to notify the cells and orchestrate a whole-body cellular response, and you are standing on the street not having a clue that this is happening, as you have now become the victim. This is because your thinking has made it about you; it is "something you did".

I used to find myself thinking that way a lot of the time, until I learned how the brain really works, and I learned that if I continued to think this way over a sustained period of time, it was going to make me very sick and potentially kill me.

But then I started to take a moment to write down what I was thinking and feeling in those moments and what the roots of those thoughts and emotions were. With that understanding I could rewrite the thoughts to challenge the negative thinking. Then, over time, this became easier and easier to do because I built up a pattern of positive thinking (not for the sake of purely just thinking positive) so that the positivity became more of an automatic reflex.

This process is a written form of a practice that I often used with people who came to me to talk about their difficulties: a method I call "Uncover, Discover, Recover". The amazing thing that I discovered is that the brain just doesn't' store our memories; it also stores the feelings associated with those memories, particularly if we have never processed these memories and they are suppressed deep in the Red Zone.

So, when something in our present environment (through our five senses) taps into a memory, it also reignites the feelings that went along with that memory and the original experience.

In a therapeutic setting a person might tell me of childhood experiences of her father arriving home from work and shouting at her and her mother, and while she is relating this to me, she starts to cry.

What she has done is "uncover" a painful emotion which she now has to deal with. In terms of the brain, it means the unprocessed emotion has resurfaced from the Red Zone and has arrived in the present moment, so that she is experiencing the emotion right there and then in present time.

In doing so, she can start to examine and "discover" how these memories and the belief system surrounding them have been affecting her life over the years. And if she can "discover" where this belief system is coming from, along with the behaviors and perceptions it has led to, then she can start to think critically and analyze what it really means and whether that belief system actually reflects the reality of the world. That process brings the experience into the Blue Zone and she can then move forward in her life.

That is the reprogramming and subsequently the "recovery" because she can see a separation between the original events and the emotions, the feelings and the behaviors that have stemmed from them, and how she wants to respond in the future when such memories spring up.

The same writing exercises work with any of the roles or personas we learned in childhood, or with any emotional situation you might find yourself in and struggling to understand.

If you are a Joker and you are writing, "I'm great fun to be around and I am the life and soul of the party, but at the end of the day my need to entertain everybody else leaves me feeling a bit empty and alone", then you can follow it by thinking and writing other ways that you can belong in your relationships and your community. This means recognizing and becoming aware that you can still make people laugh if you are doing it just for the sake of doing it, rather than from feeling a duty to make everybody else happy.

And it means recognizing that you have a lot of other things to offer, and that you belong in other healthier ways, too.

If you recognize yourself in the role of the Lost Child—maybe you have never found your voice or learned to stand up for yourself—you can use it to recognize that you do have something to say and a story to tell, and through writing you can help yourself find and develop that voice.

If you are a Rebel, you can start by asking yourself whether you really feel well both mentally and physically, because this role typically comes with a great deal of anger and resentment. If the answer is no, you can use your writing to separate your emotions from any harmful behavior and start to develop healthier behaviors which align with the kind of person that you really want to be.

If you are feeling lost or out of control, it's a highly effective way to pause and take stock of your thoughts. If you are feeling burdened or undervalued, you can dig into the deeper experiences that might be causing that and work towards realizing that you do not have to make other people's decisions for them or always lead the way. If you have always been thought of as the Baby, you can move yourself to the head of your own pack.

Whatever it is you want to change about your way of looking at the world, you just have to realize that you are not stuck with what I call the so called, prescribed script, the one that you adopted through your faulty programming in childhood.

"

The important thing to remember is that you cannot change the past. You cannot undo events that have happened in your life, and you can't really change the memories of them or erase the emotions that you felt at the time.

But you can change your present and future experiences. You can take ownership of them and learn from them, and that means taking responsibility for how you behave when these past memories and emotions are triggered. It means that you can no longer blame your parents or anyone else, because you have the power to respond.

That is reprogramming and true recovery.

This is reality. Do not take my word for it; examine it, discover and decide for yourself. Do not overanalyze it, for over analysis creates paralysis. Examine it, make a decision, and then act.

It is so empowering to know that we can take control of our own lives. That we have a big say over our health and wellness. That peace, contentment, real happiness, are there for all of us.

Most of us in this incredibly consumeristic, capitalistic world that we have collectively created, sleepwalk ourselves through a meaningless life, often full of fear, and then die.

A lot of people just examine life in a very superficial or academic, cognitive way, and then decide that life is just about chaos and random choice and is ultimately meaningless. That is not true. I cannot overemphasize how much control we have over our own life, if we just take the time to examine and reflect. This is what I have been learning about with great benefit from these 48 Acts.

You get just one shot at this wonderful event called life. Arm yourself with all this important knowledge and understanding, and give life the great blast that it and you deserve.

The famous scientist Marie Curie had a great saying that really summed up this Act for me:

"Nothing in life is to be feared, it is only to be understood.

Now is the time to understand more, so that we may fear less".

ॐ 6 ॐ

Come to the realization that:
    "Life is full of suffering",
    "Your life is not about you",
"There is a power greater than you".

When I first saw these statements in the first Sixteen Axioms, I will admit that I found them to be challenging. This, I'm sure, is because most of what I had believed to be true had been programmed in my brain from a very young age, and I never had the ability to be able to examine these thoughts and teachings that I am sure were given to me by parents, guardians and teachers with the best of intentions.

I, like most people, had been programmed from a young age to expect people and the world around me to behave in a certain way. I had my own expectations of how the world should be, and how I should be in the world. That is all good in the short term, but what happens when my very narrow beliefs and expectations are not met? I get anxious. The more anxious I get, the more I get locked into my very narrow understanding of myself and the world around me, it becomes me against them, and the cycle continues.

Having gone through thirty-eight Acts, my view of both myself and the world has completely changed. It is not that the world around me changed; it is I who has changed, and interestingly as I changed, the world around me has changed as well.

This program taught me to broaden my thoughts and my understanding of what is happening in the world. I do not believe everything I hear and read anymore. I learned to examine and critically evaluate. I constantly seek the truth now, even my own truth.

"Life is full of suffering."

There is no escaping the fact that life is full of suffering. Our life is ultimately about loss, and our wellness is measured by how well we relate to, and adapt to, these inevitable losses. People will get sick and people will die. That truth is incontrovertible, a fact of life. I spent my entire life living with a fear of getting sick and dying, and guess what the consequences of that were? I did not enjoy life; fear took over.

Now, thanks to this program, I have gone full circle. I now no longer fear death. I know that someday I am going to die, and this realization has challenged me to live a life full of purpose and meaning, and to assist other people to live lives full of purpose and meaning also.

I do not have an attachment to loss anymore, though I know that loss is inevitable. But I now know that I have the tools to work through those moments when they come.

I have also learned on this journey that due to the greed and lack of awareness of humans, there is great suffering on the planet that need not be.

We should always be aware of people who live their lives in great suffering caused by conflict, war, natural disasters, and man's inhumanity to man.

We should never lose our compassion, empathy and love for those people who are in a worse position than ourselves. The world is sadly deficient in kindness at all levels at the moment. These are the things we should be striving to achieve, and these in much greater doses would make the world more habitable than it is at this moment.

"Your life is not about you."

As I mentioned previously, I never thought that my life was about me. My life was about fixing everybody else and solving all the problems of the world. How could it have been about me?

But more and more, as I worked my way through these Acts, I began to see that it was all about me. It was about escaping my pain, it was about wanting people to like me, it was about me having to know everything. As I was not aware of this, I did not realize the damage that this was causing to both myself and the nearest and dearest around me.

More and more as I look around me, I can see that me culture. It is about how I look, about how educated I am, the car I drive, the location I live in, my nails, my hair, my social network likes, the vested interests of life, what's in it for me, how will this affect me. We are a society that has become besotted with ourselves.

Something else that needs to be understood here is how the increased levels of anxiety are feeding into this me culture. I do hope that in all that has been written up to now that we are getting a greater sense of the impact that anxiety is having on the world.

Remember that anxiety is all about survival in the short term, so automatically, the more anxious the individual becomes, the more they retreat into themselves for survival. Left unchecked, over a sustained period of time, we will lose empathy and compassion for others.

.The more anxious we become, the more time we spend in the Red Zone and incrementally over time we disconnect from the Blue Zone. We are losing the Blue Zone functions of empathy and compassion, and that means the more it becomes about me the less we will care about others. That is an indisputable fact. You do not have to believe me; go examine the research.

"There is a power greater than you."

I have learned through this program that there is indeed a power greater than me. I have also learned that it is not actually the God that I thought it was. In my Christian upbringing I was always taught about this all-powerful God, full of love and compassion, who was always there by our side even if we were sinners. As you can imagine, this was very difficult to reconcile when I was just a helpless child who was sexually abused by a middle man with power, control and recognition and who acted as a go-between, between both myself and this God.

In much more recent times, I happened to be attending a funeral mass of a friend, when the officiating priest asked us all to pray for the "Christians who were suffering and dying in the war in Syria".

This was an eye-opening moment for me, as it was the first time that I could see how the ideologies of religions have almost destroyed the world. Here was this priest (a young man) inviting prayer only for his flock, and completely blind to the fact that members of other flocks were suffering and dying in Syria at the same time.

This is what the ideologies of religion have created, an us against them culture that does nothing to engender unity and compassion among humans; and what is worse, they have used the ideas of their God to create conflict and wars.

To me power and energy are the same. If you are hooked into the greater power, you are hooked into the greater energy. It is energy that makes the world function. Every single part of you, me, plants, trees, the world, the solar system, the galaxy, and the universe is made up of energy of one form or another. It does not have a name, it is unknowable. We are just energy, and it is important to be able to simplify it like this. This energy is all around us; you can see it, you can feel it, it is within us.

We are all a tiny grouping of energies in our bodies, and we are exactly the same as everybody else. We are part of this greater energy (God) in the real sense, because we are the same energy.

When we are in a very unwell state, all our polarities are misaligned. So, if we are in the Red Zone for too long, we will have negative energy. If we are in the Blue Zone for too long, we will have positive energy. But we cannot be positive all the time as that is not realistic; we have to understand the negative energy, as it is about our survival. It is a balance. If energy is balanced all will be well. As we try to become more aware, we become more aligned and in tune with the universe.

The more open and sincere and true we are, the more aligned we will become with the power/energy/God of the universe, and it will reveal itself more to us. All we have to do is act as if there is a power greater than us.

7
"COME TO SEE THAT KNOWLEDGE, LEADING TO UNDERSTANDING, WILL LEAD YOU TO AWARENESS."

As we are encouraged through the Acts to gain more self-knowledge, this Act has taught me that there are different types of knowledge. In the main we have cognitive knowledge, but we also have experiential knowledge, intuitive knowledge and gut-knowing.

The real gift that we bring to the table is our understanding of the lived life that we have experienced. The more cognitive information, e.g., the science of how the body and brain work that I was learning about, the more I was able to apply this learning to my life experiences, both good and bad.

As we become more open and truer to ourselves and as we begin to deprogram, we begin to realize that it was not just a simple thing of good or bad. In the beginning I was a little bit picky in that I was only writing about the good things, and I had this idea that if I could eventually find enough good things, the bad things might not seem so bad.

But I soon realized I was only fooling myself and not being honest with myself. I discovered that I was really good at talking about my lived experiences, but I was not that good at owning them. Owning these experiences is much more difficult.

It was really easy to talk about the things that happened to me and the impact that they had on my life, but the hardest part was to talk about how my behavior impacted other people's lives.

I eventually came around to the thinking that it was not helpful to see experiences as good or bad. I learned to see them simply as experiences. That is all they were, experiences, and they were neither good or bad, as each experience teaches us something about ourselves. Indeed, it is often the most painful and difficult experiences that teach us the most about ourselves, if we are honest enough to own them.

As I began to have a more open dialogue with myself, I also began to see people and the world in a different way, in a much more compassionate light.

Instead of just seeing people's behaviors and judging them on their behaviors, I began to see the person behind the behavior. Behind every maladaptive practice there is a human being that is hurting, is disconnected from themselves, and does not have awareness. That is not to say that we accept people's behavior, that is not what I am talking about; no, what I am talking about is that when we comment on and judge other people, it is often a disowned part of ourselves that we are talking about.

When we can begin to see people in this way, we are able to walk away rather than react to their behavior, and allow ourselves to feel a little bit of compassion and empathy for them. This is ultimately good for us, and that little bit of kindness and understanding can often be what the other person needs, not judgement.

Experiential, gut and intuitive knowing and understanding are the key to awareness.

8
"WITH COMPLETE HONESTY EXAMINE ALL BEHAVIORS AND MALADAPTIVE PRACTICES, IDENTIFYING ALL SUCH BEHAVIORS THAT ARE LEADING TO SELF-HARM, DESTRUCTION AND UNHAPPINESS."

The more we learn about ourselves, the further along the road to awareness and wellness we progress. Learning to be honest with myself and others continues to be a challenge, but at least I am aware of it now. Continually examining all of my past and present behaviors and maladaptive practices are getting easier. I just keep writing them down and challenging the thoughts that go with them.

I can see now that this will be an ongoing challenge. If it took the best part of a lifetime to begin to become unwell, I would be foolish to think that I will get well in a short space of time. I now know that I won't. It will come with the consistency and persistence of doing the work on a daily basis; there is no quick fix.

Being honest with myself is really difficult. I spent my life looking at and being addicted to fixing other people's pain as an escape from dealing with my own pain. For that reason, in particular, I can often feel unworthy about spending time managing my own pain, and I have to work particularly hard to be kind and gentle with myself and not allow myself to indulge in pangs of guilt.

At this particular junction of following this program of recovery, I have come to realize that guilt is a luxury that I cannot afford.

I can beat myself up forever over things that I have done, or things that I did not do; but that is all pointless. All that will do is keep me stuck in the past and mired in the quicksand of regrets and resentments.

I have learned now that it is as it is; I can only deal with where I am now and keep moving forward one step at a time by continuing to work on this program, which is serving me well. I now know it will continue to serve me well in the future.

9
"DECIDE TO CHANGE ALL SUCH HARMFUL BEHAVIORS".

I have had a great breakthrough in my own head in recent times. I now know that I am worth repairing, that I am not all bad, that I am no better or no worse than anybody else.

I also know that I have been doing my best, with the best of intentions. I was just this damaged young child who had adopted the persona of the good child, who wanted to fix everybody and wanted everybody to love me. Without awareness, of course, I had no conscious knowledge of the mistakes I was making. That is not to say that I am not responsible for those mistakes, and I still have to take personal responsibility, which I have been doing.

I have reached a good level of awareness now, and I have come to the realization that:

I cannot fix the world,
I cannot make people like me, and
I am as important as anybody else, no more, no less.

I am not controlled by the problems of the world anymore. I am aware of them, but I know I cannot fix them. Being aware in this way allows me to have more compassion and empathy for myself and for others.

I am learning to be a lot more resilient.

Resilience is the ability to see failure not as something that we should hold on to, but as an opportunity to move forward accepting that failure is a part of our journey through life.

Resilience, to me, involves three essential elements. I call them the triple A rating for wellness in life, and they are:

ATTITUDE ACCEPTANCE AWARENESS

All of these elements would prove to be key factors that assisted me on my ongoing journey to recovery.

10

"RESOLVE TO LEAVE THE PAST BEHIND, AS IT NOW HAS NO POWER OVER YOU. CEASE TO IDENTIFY WITH IT, AND INSTEAD LIVE IN THE PRESENT, LOOKING FORWARD TO A HAPPY FUTURE."

I spent most of my life living in the past. I was not aware of this, and believed that in the way I was living my life I was actually dealing with the past.

The paradox here, of course, is that the more I tried to run away from the past, the more the past remained in the present. The natural consequence of this was that I was never happy in the present and constantly worried about the future.

The past is always present, that is an incontrovertible truth. It has to be; remember that our Red Zone is primarily there to remember our past experiences and instincts, which allows us to survive in the present. Without this happening, every time we put our hand in the fire we would be burned, as our Red Zone would not remember to pull it out.

Our Red Zone never forgets. All of our life experiences and memories are stored there, and they go back through generations to a time when the first human organism appeared. That is the way it has to be. It does not separate our memories and experiences, because it holds on to everything for survival. The separation of these memories and experiences is up to us.

That is the work we are doing with this program. By becoming aware, by examining, by evaluating, we will know what to do with these memories and their associated emotions when they pop up unannounced.

That is the real recovery, because from now on when these bad feelings suddenly appear we will not be afraid of them. We will understand them, and we will just breathe and allow them to be. We will not resort to maladaptive behaviors and practices anymore, because we now know that these uncomfortable feelings are not to be feared; they are just to be understood, they are our friend. They will empower us to go on and be the best we can be for ourselves and for others.

This is the power of understanding the Blue Zone/Red Zone concept.

The Red Zone is about keeping us safe in the present. The Blue Zone is about planning for the future. When these two are in harmony, this is where real happiness lies, and if we continue with this program the way we are, we will get there. That is guaranteed, as it is based on absolute fact and reality.

A word of warning here though, and this is purely from my own personal experience. Some of the language that is very often used by the media and the wellness industry was not helpful for me on my journey of understanding, in particular the phrases like "letting go" and "seeking closure", and the one that the media really loves: "victims".

I was constantly advised to "let go", and that it was only by letting go that I would become well. The problem was that I was not quite sure what it was I was supposed to let go in the first place, and nobody else seemed to know either.

"Closure" was another term often used. The idea was that I could not move on in my life without closure; further suggesting that unless my abuser was brought through the court system, I would never have closure.

What happens, though (as in my case), if the abuser is deceased? Does this mean that I will never have closure?

Closure and letting go do not mean that the past is gone. The past will never be gone; the past is always present, because our Red Zone always holds on to everything for survival. But having awareness does mean that when painful moments come (and they will), and we feel a wave of pain and hurt and sorrow washing over us, we can learn how to manage it. The danger of not doing so is that all this pain and anxiety will be stored not just in the Red Zone but also in the form of cellular memories, which can cause the mind and body to become sick.

Remember that when we continually process things in a negative way, our Red Zone response keeps sending messages to our cells for a "fight, flight or freeze" response, while also tapping into our cellular memories in the process. If we live our life in this constant cycle without any awareness, the ultimate unease and imbalance creates disease, which makes us sick and can even kill us.

I do not see myself as a victim; yes, I was victimized in my life, just like many others have been. Thinking of ourselves as a victim may initially feel empowering, and other people will want to steal and manipulate our narrative to create their own selfish narrative, but this gets stale very quickly. Amend your story of unfairness to look for the hidden benefits that have made us wiser and more secure. Celebrate yourself as a conqueror, rather than a victim. Understand your past, embrace it, move on in harmony with it, and marvel at how the fear that you have lived your life in, dissipates over time.

11

"TAKE RESPONSIBILITY FOR ALL YOUR ACTIONS PAST AND PRESENT, IRRESPECTIVE OF WHAT THEY ARE, AND CEASE TO BLAME OTHERS. DECIDE TO GET RID OF ALL RESENTMENTS, JUSTIFIED OR UNJUSTIFIED, SEEING THEM FOR THE POISON OF THE SOUL THAT THEY REALLY ARE".

In this Act I learned that once we begin to take responsibility for our actions past and present, we learn that what we did in the past we did in ignorance and unawareness, and we are truly sorry for it. We also learn that what was done to us in the past was often done out of ignorance. We cease to blame others irrespective of what they have done to us, as the only person that suffers when we blame others is ourselves; but we do attribute to them that they have done and what is wrong. We do all of this with a desire to be well and to learn to live in the real reality of the world.

Facing reality can be emotionally trying in the short term, but life-saving later on. The key is not to get stuck with it in the short term, and to trust that no matter how dire the situation may seem right now, we can survive and thrive. Because the moment we accept the burdens that we have been given, the door often opens to another way of seeing things and subsequently doing things. It is no good focusing our life on how we think things should be or could be—that will only keep us living in the Red Zone and make us sick. But if we can accept our life as it is, then we can do something about it.

Accepting is not chickening out, by the way. Chickening out means not making a decision at all, whereas accepting our situation means making a commitment to do so.

Once we have made that commitment, we have given ourselves options that we hopefully can move forward with.

This sort of acceptance requires a substantial amount of relinquishing of past hurts, of people to blame, and of expectations that the world owes us anything at all. It also requires forgiveness both of others and of ourselves.

As we learn to forgive others, we learn to forgive ourselves. The more we can forgive others, the more we can forgive ourselves. The more we can free ourselves from the chains of hate, the more we can become well, as self-hate is the hate that binds us most.

Forgiveness is not easy. It is easier to hold resentments, to seek vengeance. It is easier to live in the past and blame others for where we are in our lives today. At best vengeance is useless; it will not change the things that happened to us. It can't delete the wrongs we have suffered. At worst vengeance perpetuates the cycle of hate. It keeps the hate alive. This is where evil resides in the world, in our blame. We blame minority groups, we blame somebody of a different color, a different sexual orientation, someone wealthier, someone poorer.

We blame what people have done to us in a personal sense. We blame our parents, our brothers, our sisters, our aunt, our uncle, our friends. We blame anybody and everybody. But deep down we really blame ourselves.

When we seek vengeance, even nonviolent vengeance, we are just going around in circles and never moving forward. Vengeance does not set us free.

With this new learning fresh in my consciousness, I stood outside the door of an old house in my town of birth, and forgave him (even though he was long dead, I had been holding on to the pain in my heart). This had nothing to do with him; it was something I did for me. I was relinquishing, releasing the part of myself that had spent most of my life exerting the mental and spiritual energy to keep my abuse in chains. To forgive is to grieve—for what happened in my life, for what didn't happen in my life.

Forgiveness and acceptance are two of the most difficult things that I ever had to do, as it meant focusing on my own mistakes and imperfections as a human. The most difficult thing we will ever have to do is face our own truth. I can beat myself up for the rest of my life over decisions that I have made. Or I can acknowledge that the most important decision is not the one I made when I was lonely, unaware, desperately wanting to belong and to be heard, desperate to make a difference in the world, desperate to feel any other identity than a hurt, dirty little nine-year-old boy.

Through this Act I have now found an identity that is truly my own. I had to learn to let go of my resentments, whether they were justified or not. As this Act teaches us, they are just a poison of the soul, and the only soul that is being poisoned is our own. As the Buddha said, "Holding onto anger is like holding on to a hot coal looking for someone to throw it at, and you are the one who is getting burned".

12
"RESOLVING TO BECOME YOUR TRUE INTEGRATED AUTHENTIC SELF, YOU WILL ENDEAVOR AS MUCH AS POSSIBLE TO MAKE GOOD THE HARM YOU HAVE CAUSED TO OTHERS IN A THOUGHTFUL WAY".

It has taken me a long time to come to the reality of this Act, especially for me who was the ultimate fixer, the ultimate Florence Nightingale, wanting to help others just so that I could feel better about myself.

Of course, there were times when I did feel better about myself, when I helped somebody, when I gave things to people, when I sat up all night listening to people share their darkest moments. But they were only fleeting glances of feeling good, and ultimately, I had to work harder to achieve any crumb of kindness toward myself.

Now that I live in reality and awareness, I can see all of this so clearly. It was always about me. This is not to say that other people were not helped, of course they were. The damage in a lot of cases was that I did too much for people and often disempowered them from finding their own truth and pathway in life.

One great example of something that happened to me really encapsulates what this Act is telling us.

While working my way through this Act I identified a friend of a number of years back, whom I would have caused great hurt due to my behavior and lack of awareness. I contacted this friend, and we arranged to meet up. I acknowledged my poor behavior of the past and offered my sincere apologies.

My friend would not accept my apology and admonished me for what had happened. He then subsequently stormed off.

I was devastated and felt that I had been set back substantially in my recovery. It was only when I read this Act a number of times that I could see what had happened. When I was approaching my friend to apologize, I had an expectation that he was going to be so pleased for me, congratulate me on how well I was doing and tell me that I was great and how proud of me he was. Boy did I get that wrong.

Firstly, it was not, as this Act points out, my true authentic self that approached my friend. It was the old me wanting to be acknowledged and appreciated. I learned the value of this Act the hard way.

I do not help others anymore just to make me feel better. It is not about me; it is simply the right thing to do.

❧ 13 ☙
"LEARN UNCONDITIONAL ACCEPTANCE OF HOW YOU WERE, OF WHAT HAPPENED TO YOU, OF HOW YOU HURT OTHERS, AND FORGIVE YOURSELF; OF HOW YOU WERE HURT BY OTHERS, AND FORGIVE THEM ALL."

It is often quite startling how awareness changes the way we see and experience the world around us, and that includes the people in our lives right now, or our parents who have died.

Awareness, as I have been learning through these Acts, is important for wellness. But I am also learning that the early stages of awareness can be very painful, as it makes things very real and raw. In the same way acceptance is very difficult, as it challenges us to look at the bigger picture of our life story.

For most of my life I just saw my mother as the mental patient and my father as the alcoholic, and would often ponder whether our lives would have been any better if we had not been afflicted with parents who had such difficulties and challenges. In a sense I was still holding some blame and resentment towards my parents for the difficulties I had in my life, but through this program and in particular this Act I was becoming more aware and working on it.

This Act really challenged me to look at how I was in my relationship with my parents and see if there was ways I could have behaved and acted differently. Of course, there was, and in particular I could have been much kinder towards my father. I had spent most of my life blaming their difficulties for some of my difficulties, but never until now had I looked at how I had behaved towards them.

This Act really challenged me to acknowledge and accept that there were things that I did which I am sure must have hurt my parents, my father in particular. Forgiveness, I discovered, was a two-way street. I had to be willing to accept the things that happened with my parents and also be willing to forgive them for the hurts that I perceived they had perpetrated on me. However, at the same time I had to forgive myself for allowing these perceived hurts to go so deep, and also how I in turn acted towards other people, in particular my parents, as a consequence of these hurts.

Often when we arrive in awareness, we believe that other people should be aware as well. That is not the case.

In the words of a very wise person,

"Forgive them, for they know not what they do".

❦ 14 ❧
"YOU WILL CONTINUE EVERY DAY TO WORK ON YOURSELF AND SELF-REFLECT. TO REALIZE THE DIVINE SPARK OF GREATNESS WITHIN YOU. TO LOVE YOURSELF AS YOU TRULY ARE, ACCEPTING THAT THERE IS LOVE AND TRUTH IN THE WORLD THAT IS UNALIENABLE."

For the first time in my lifetime, I can say that my life is my own. I am no longer disempowered by my fears; I have the power to choose. I have not been radicalized, for nobody or nothing controls me. I have arrived at this peace of mind myself.

Paddy Rafter's *48 Acts Towards a Different Way of Living* did not tell me what to do. What it did do is that it offered me a template and a pathway to explore and examine the world for myself, in a true and honest way. It has helped me to live in a world of truth and reality, rather than of fear and pretense.

On a close examination of the world, it is fair to say that it is really struggling at the moment. But the world is only struggling because people are struggling. The world is just a macrocosm of the microcosm of the individual.

The sad thing is that many people already know this, and feel that everything is meaningless, useless, and that there is nothing they can do.

Yes, there is something that we can do. We can do a lot. Remember that we are just energy. We all have this divine spark of energy within us; we must have, for if we didn't, we would be dead. The problem for most of us is that it manifests as a negative energy because of the way we are living in the world now.

I spoke a little earlier about our default position being negative, particularly during really anxious times as our negative Red Zone is all about survival, and if we are spending most of our lives now in the Red Zone, well then, we will constantly experience the world in a threatening way (negatively).

It is so easy to get caught up in the constant 24-hour media onslaught of all the bad that is happening in the world. To a certain extent that is true; the world is in a difficult place and the negativity is palpable. We can so easily get locked into trying to change people and change the outcome of events. What I have learned in this Act is that we cannot do this. We cannot change other people. But what we have to do, as this Act asks us to, is to continually work on ourselves, examine and self-reflect. It is only by consistently doing this that we can, over time, effect some change, as the positive polarity can attract and create positivity in others.

I have learned through constant examination, as this Act requests of us, that despite all the negativity and despite all the real difficulties that are out there, there is also an even greater abundance of love and truth. It is just that we have to work and search much harder for them, as they do not make the headlines.

Through this Act I realized that the best way I could ever make a difference and be a part of creating healing in the world was by being well myself. Through constant self-examination I learned to love myself as I truly am.

If we can do this and keep working from the inside out, we will arrive at a point where we will love ourselves, but we will love our neighbor as well. If we humans have introduced evil into the world, we can also bring back the love that is already there, for it is just in hiding.

15

"HAVING GAINED MUCH GREATER UNDERSTANDING AND REALIZING THAT THERE IS A FORCE MUCH GREATER THAN US OUT THERE, WILL HELP US WHEN ALL ELSE FAILS, IF WE JUST ASK. HAVING KNOWN SO MUCH PAIN AND TRAUMA, WE WILL KNOW THAT HUMILITY IN ITSELF IS NOT HUMILIATION, AND THUS WE WILL LOOSEN THE CHAINS THAT BIND US, AND SET OURSELVES FREE."

A number of years ago I was publicly humiliated in the cruelest and most unimaginable way possible. I descended into depths of darkness and despair that words could not explain. This public humiliation completely fractured my already fragile ego and false self and catapulted me into having to confront that darkest and most hidden part of myself that I had spent a lifetime running away from.

Ironically, around that time I also came in contact with Paddy Rafter and his work, *The 48 Acts Towards a New Way of Living*.

I have documented throughout the last forty-six Acts my incremental journey of the almost surrendering of my past life into the "The New Way" as outlined in this inspirational work.

Throughout this journey I have not been what I call "religiosified", or ideologized, indoctrinated, or coerced into seeing and experiencing the world in any particular way. All I received was a "Way" to experience the world in a very holistic, honest and examined way by being able to come to terms, at my own time and pace, with the reality of my own story of life.

There is an expression that goes, "You have kept the good wine until now", and in the best tradition of all the great storytellers, Paddy has kept the best wine until last.

"Having known so much pain and trauma, you will know that humility in itself is not humiliation, and thus you will loosen the chains that bind you and set yourself free".

As I have just mentioned, I suffered the most incredible and painful public humiliation that you could imagine. This invoked in me the most horrendous feelings of shame and guilt, two very corrosive emotions, and I thought I would never recover. But I did, thanks to this incredible work of Paddy Rafter that I was privileged to be the first to experience.

My greatest learning has come in this Act. The humiliation that I had encountered has now, forty-seven Acts later, brought me to a place of peace, contentment and humility.

My humiliation has become my humility, because I found the courage through this program to confront the truths of my humiliation. To accept what was mine, but also to reject what was not mine, to totally examine my life in an honest way, to work from the inside out, and ultimately to accept myself as I truly am.

In a strange, bizarre, but wonderful way, the acceptance of my humiliation has led me on a path to humility and humbleness. This in turn has allowed me, for the first time in almost fifty-four years, to loosen the chains that have always bound me, and subsequently set myself free.

16
"GET INTO REALITY, BECOME AWARE."

Having reached the end of these Acts, I have discovered that there is no end. What I got from these Acts was this idea that once we get to number forty-eight, we go right back to number one and start again.

Getting into and staying in reality will always be challenging, in particular in a world where there is no verification of the truth. I have learned throughout this program that being aware is not always a nice place. Being aware challenges us to stay with the reality of the suffering that will inevitably arrive on our doorstep. When this happens to you, do not run away from it, do not isolate yourself, just learn to be with it and not to be afraid.

I have learned through this program that reality and awareness are like two great soulmates. They will never let us down. They will hold us in a safe place until the darkness passes, and it will. This is because we will have learned to trust the moment.

Always remember we are never on our own; we are all just energy, and we are all the same. We are all a part of the same energy, the energy of the universe.

As the final Act says:

"We are the song, the singer, and that which is sung. We have become aware".

FOOTNOTE

When I set out on this journey of writing this book to try to disseminate how Paddy Rafter's 48 Acts were of such immense value to me, and also how they could help others, I never in my wildest dreams would have imagined the positive impact they would have on my life.

Though many people in time to come will read these 48 Acts and try to understand them and interpret them in different ways, I believe I have a unique insight and understanding that nobody else could possibly have.

This is because of the hundreds and hundreds of hours I have spent sitting with Paddy and listening to him, as he said the same things hundreds of times, over and over again, in order to bring his work to this level of excellence.

My understanding, interpretation, integration and the subsequent development of Paddy's ideas will always stand unique. The reason for this is because "I was there". It was a privilege for me to have been a part of this journey, and I know fundamentally that anybody who takes time to partake of the journey of the 48 Acts will feel the same sense of privilege and gratitude that I now experience on a daily basis.

www.ingramcontent.com/pod-product-compliance
Lightning Source LLC
Chambersburg PA
CBHW020138130526
44591CB00030B/109